Angela's Angels Revisited: Psychic Detective

Angela McGhee

New Edition 2018
Previously Published and distributed in the United States of America by:
Hay House, Inc., PO Box 5100, Carlsbad, CA 92018-5100. Tel.: (1) 760 431 7695 or

(800) 654 5126; Fax: (1) 760 431 6948 or (800) 650 5115.
www.hayhouse.com

Published and distributed in Australia by:
Hay House Australia Ltd, 18/36 Ralph St, Alexandria NSW 2015.
Tel.: (61) 2 9669 4299; Fax: (61) 2 9669 4144. www.hayhouse.com.au

Published and distributed in the Republic of South Africa by:
Hay House SA (Pty), Ltd, PO Box 990, Witkoppen 2068. Tel./Fax: (27) 11 467 8904. www.hayhouse.co.za

Published and distributed in India by:
Hay House Publishers India, Muskaan Complex, Plot No.3, B-2, Vasant Kunj, New Delhi – 110 070. Tel.: (91) 11 4176 1620; Fax: (91) 11 4176 1630. www.hayhouse.co.in

Distributed in Canada by:
Raincoast, 9050 Shaughnessy St, Vancouver, BC V6P 6E5. Tel.: (1) 604 323 7100; Fax: (1) 604 323 2600

© Angela McGhee, 2009

Previously published by Author House, 2007, ISBN 978-1-

4343-4720-6 The moral rights of the author have been

asserted.

All rights reserved. No part of this book may be reproduced by any mechanical, photographic or electronic process, or in the form of a phonographic recording; nor may it be stored in a retrieval system, transmitted or otherwise be copied for public or private use, other than for 'fair use' as brief quotations embodied in articles and reviews, without prior written permission of the publisher.

The author of this book does not dispense medical advice or prescribe the use of any technique as a form of treatment for physical or medical problems without the advice of a physician, either directly or indirectly. The intent of the author is only to offer information of a general nature to help you in your quest for emotional
and spiritual wellbeing. In the event you use any of the information in this book for yourself, which is your constitutional right, the author and the publisher assume no responsibility for your actions.

A catalogue record for 2009 edtion book is available from the British Library.

ISBN 978-1-84850-085-3

Angela Angels Revisited 2018
ISBN-13:978-1540774279

ISBN-10:1540774279

Photo credits: Special thanks
Photos on pages 151 and 1521: David and Sheila McKenna
Photo on page 256: Joan Maxwell
Page 110 Family of Michael Sheehan
Page 324 Kerry Baker
All other photos: author and author's family

Angela's Angels Revisited:

Psychic Detective

Angela McGhee

Contents

Foreword – Jules McCarthy……………………….. vii

Introduction ....
REVISTED………………………………………………………………….
Born a Psychic Child 26
Grandmother's Visit 38
Teen Years.. 42
Grandmother's Orders 48
Madeleine's Macca Madness..................................... 54
Mother's Intuition.. 62
Past, Present and Future... 78
Sensitive Children.. 82
Spiritualism and Me 88
John's Rainbow 94
Balloons………………………………………………………………..102
Sister Bridget and Sister Theresa 113
Murder and Crime... 127
Baz's Story 153
Murder via Text... 171
DoubleCase……………………………………………………………175
Missing (in Spirit) 181
Tell the World 187
Angels, Heroes, Saints and Sinners 206
Nell………………………………………………………………………..215
George……………………………………………………………………223

Oh Lord!	228
Linda	234
Ozzy- Epilogue	243
Clare's Shamrock	255
Falklands Hero – A Soldier's Tale	271
Marian	275
Revisited II	296
Two Crosses	307
Beliefs	324
Afterword	329

Foreword

In the middle of a crowded theatre audience, at a show I was never supposed to be actually at, Angela McGhee gave me 15 minutes with the grandfather I lost when I was just seven years old. Granddad was my world, and post-operative shock took him away in a heartbeat one day while I was at junior school.

As she stood directly in front of me and asked, 'Where's Julie?', Angela carefully described Granddad's hand-knitted cardigan with the leather-covered buttons and paisley silk scarf to the last detail, even the angle of his trilby hat, his dodgy sense of humour and his passion for pigeon-keeping.

Unlike so many other mediums I've seen work, Angela can give you relevant names and answer questions when she is talking to the people you have lost. And they're specific things – not just random sentences. My granddad wanted to know where my curls had gone. In the middle of the stage Angela described how my tight dark brown ringlets had grown all the way past my bum when he'd left me. And she was right – though you wouldn't know it from the highlighted spiky short crop I straighten daily today!

He wanted me to know that the jewellery I had, which used to belong to him, was the real thing and not a cheap copy as another relative had upset me by claiming. But I don't remember Angela ever being there when this unpleasantness was aired. Neither was she with me when I was showing my children the slope outside his house where I learned to walk while holding on to his huge foundry hands. But she knew I'd been there and what was said to my children, and that he was laughing with us at the fact that someone had knocked down his pigeon pen in the backyard and built a driveway in its place.

Suddenly you're engulfed in that special sense of love and light that promises to walk with you every mile you take without them. It's like being wrapped in your favourite jumper and fed pure nectar from the people you miss most.

Angela McGhee should be available on prescription to everyone who needs to find that special sense of closure that can only come from Spirit! Utterly priceless – the wow factor that changes your life and the way you feel about everything.

When my timer goes off in this world and they come to take me on to the next life, I know that I'll be free to have tea and crumpets once again with the man who took the slow boat to China without me when I was just seven years old.

Since meeting and working with Angela through my job as a BBC news journalist, I've been party to many events (good and bad) on the world stage that highlight her true commitment to helping and healing people through the Spirit World. Never mind the book – she needs a documentary series to be written around her work.

Jules McCarthy
BBC Journalist

Introduction

Welcome. I want to welcome you to my world, my unique world of Spirit.

I was given a gift of communication at birth, part of which is being able to communicate with those people who have 'crossed over' to the 'Other Side', the Spirit World the heavenly realms, that is. I am what some people would call a psychic medium, although in hindsight, I have been called many things but fundamentally I am a Christian woman with a 'gift' which has taken on many 'guises' for the sake of other peoples understanding but never the less, its purpose is to reach and touch many people particularly, those of little faith, or total non-believers, who in desperate situations in life, need some words of comfort, solace and understanding. .

This, my first book in my own words, is a compilation of remarkable true stories of my life's quest and its amazing events that span a period of over 40 years. I have gone to the depths of self-discovery to understand and share both my very 'humane' and spiritual experiences with you

This book describes the difficulties in coming to terms with the 'gift' that was given to me, but it was through its connection with life's struggles, traumas and tragedies that I learned about its true purpose and reason, as it eventually became my saviour. It was, and still is, totally humbling for me.

I have now shared my gift to help and heal others, and have met some wonderful people from both sides of the 'veil' – some of whom you are about to meet!

This gift has also been used to assist the police in solving cases of murder. The subject of this work has been documented in the TV series *Psychic Investigators*.

I have now begun to touch even more people's souls with my gift, on a world stage, bringing them love, hope, comfort and enlightenment – something which was prophesied for me from an early age. The gift is something that never ceases to amaze even me, and I am, and have always been, totally in awe of it. It is one of life's miracles.

These stories lay bare the first layers of my soul, which I have found it very difficult to expose. They explore my own sense and understanding of spirituality, in the hope that it helps and benefits those who are trying to grasp a meaning and true purpose to life, death and the life hereafter.

This is a semi-autobiographical book. You will find that some incidents will 'hinge' on other stories, where I have had to respect and give careful consideration to other people's thoughts and feelings. It is only through the process of healing and time that those stories will be told. It appears that each week that goes by in my life is a 'sequel' to the previous chapter.

I, like everybody else, am a spiritual being having a human experience with a story to tell. This is my first book in a series – God willing!

Love and Light,

Angela 2007

REVISITED (2018)

'Angela's Angel's is a terminology I use to express a term in relation to, not only those people here, that have touched and shaped my souls pathway but it is those numerous 'encounters' involving the people of the spirit world, that has in turn, not only made a communication but an eternal connection, that in recognition, never severs.

Just like good friends, they never forget you; they call and sometimes turn up unexpectedly, in knowing that they are welcomed and loved and that you would never refuse a request to help them in anyway too.

'Revisited' is exactly what it states; It has now been several years since compiling and documenting some of my most remarkable spiritual experiences that I have gathered whilst 'living between the two worlds' as I do.
My 'soul' has continued to develop and receive knowledge and understanding, not only on a spiritual level but a personnel level too.
Nothing stays the same in life, as it is a process of never ending changes.

Everything has to be embraced whether it is to our liking or not, for there is a 'reason' but all for a greater purpose yet to unfold.

Loved ones in spirit, whose stories I've mentioned in the first edition, their timely communications and interactions have continued intermitted and still do, often by surprise. A number of original chapters have had a 'sequel', of events with on-going spiritual intervention in some wondrous shape and form, which you will see is 'evidential' in its writing.

'Loved ones in spirit 'revisit', they continue to 'communicate' with their loved ones here, for whatever reason, not necessarily at crucial stages of their loved ones earthly life, but at lighter and wanting moments too.

They still take the opportunity to communicate and interact; never the less influencing and guiding at the same time but essentially it is with the allowance of Gods spirit, that all is possible.

As the 'writings' confirm, we all do remain spiritually connected with our loved ones in spirit and the essence of our 'relationships' continues in a spiritual sense. Caring all the same, as they once did here, in this life, as their life continues in heaven, the spirit realms.

Again, along my journey, there have been many spiritual experiences which have spanned the years, which I alone and with others have been a witness to.

Together, we have been inevitably molded and edged with perfect timing, as spirit and peoples paths have crossed, for theirs or our present purpose or that of our futures.

I now, after decades, sit comfortably in my 'spiritual' overcoat, as my 'gifts' have been acclaimed publically on Television, in the Media worldwide and by high ranking Police Detectives who, at their call, as I continue to help with Murder and Missing persons cases. Psychic Detective work is something which I reluctantly got involved with but it was a level I had to 'evolve' to, spiritually speaking. I was 'lead' into this aspect by the sheer power of spirit alone. There was never a want. The souls that have left this earth, in such terrible circumstances, whose passing has torn into the hearts of their loved ones here,. It is their troubled spirit that seems to seek me out, to find an element of peace for families and Detectives, on earth, in the form of unequivocal 'answers'.

I must say it is a fact that Police officers do call upon my Psychic 'abilities', my (Gifts) for such help, even though undercover at times. I am now regarded as an 'evidential witness' to that fact alone.

In another of my books, 'Crime Scene Psychic' opens up with my involvement in an eye-opening suspect serial killer case, which became a ground breaking 'land mark' within my very own spiritual development, alongside other cases and experiences which lead to that 'pinnacle'.

I do believe this aspect of my work is the 'Crowned' purpose of my 'gift' helping Police and families amidst such horrendous tragedies, although, being a part of it, is the most heart-breaking and humbling experiences to say the least.

My 'Gift' has also been publicly recognised and blessed by the Hierarchy of the Catholic Church and recently been tested by Scientists in Italy whilst during my visit, demonstrating, at a Science conference. What came to mind during this experimental time, was Albert Einstein's quote

~ 'The more I study science, the more I believe in God'~

Scientists are just people, who are in awe of God's wonder are they not? And being sceptic is a matter of choice.

It was these 'instrumented' experiences in particular, that helped me build my confidence to fully embrace and accept my 'Gifts' something which I had struggled with for many a decade. All these facts I mention have now been documented, those things which once 'weighed heavy' on my child- like spirit and Guides I have fully accepted, as my personal journey to self-discovery has not been an embracing or an easy passage way.

But it is my spiritual work in every aspect, that is totally humbling and invaluable, no matter who is sent to ask for my assistance in gaining a knowledge of the Afterlife and the understanding to what it can bring, which is to help complete us, as we begin to recognise we are spiritual beings in a temporary earthly existence, trying to make sense and gain solace to it all.

Again, it was with difficulty choosing which stories to add to my infantry of 'Angela's Angel's' from real life experiences, as I continue to walk with those people of the spirit world and those people here, who have been 'touched' by 'spirit' on my journey.

Their spiritual stories become a 'message' that only 'messengers' would bring.
For these are my 'Angels'- who I have given recognition to, that now have 'earned' and gained entry to 'Angela's Angels', my Award winning book, that is now 'ever expanding,' with those, heavenly and earthly 'Angels' that will be entombed, forever in the 'written' works of my daily life.

The experiences are something that people find nothing less than enrapturing, or just simply fascinating, guaranteed to grab your heart and soul, to give you thought and to help you 'seek'.

There are many more memorable stories to be written in time, as a never ending backlog of 'messages' are being created and acrued along my journey.

We must remember, we, each other, the universe, the heavenly realms, are all one of God, we are all connected without doubt and it is in true Faith and Spirituality that we shall begin to understand.

I will continue to write to give 'evidence' that Spirit, our connection of 'love' is combined within a universal 'energy force' that has God within and at its Helm.

We must take time to 'consider' life and be Kind.

Yours, in eternal gratitude.

Peace & Love.......... Angela

Born a Psychic Child

It was as if my Guardian Angel had been appointed their first task and set to work almost immediately on the day I was born. My birth itself was difficult, so I've been told. I actually died. For a while it was debatable whether I would live or not. For my first few moments on Earth, my spirit hovered between the two worlds. This may have been an indicator of what was to follow. I believe I was born a 'channel'. I was born the seventh child. But not the seventh child of the seventh child, as I'm often asked!

The events surrounding my birth were actually pinpointed on my astrological chart, which has recently been drawn up by an elderly professional astrologist called Trixie. I met her when she came to visit me for a private sitting, in which she received a beautiful communication from her late husband,

George. It was during her sitting that I heard the first words from George's spirit: 'Astrology, Astrology, Astrology!' I asked Trixie what this meant. She laughed as she replied, 'Yes, he would say that, as I have studied astrology for over 50 years. It was, and still is, my passion!'

A

After her sitting, she was so pleased that she pleaded for my permission to study my astrological birth chart: 'I bet it would be fascinating to do! Please may I? I would truly love to.' Somewhat reluctantly, I gave her my details. When it was completed a week or so later, we met up and, as she handed me the chart, she remarked about the 'crisis' that surrounded my birth and also the so-called gift or ability that had been highlighted throughout the years. These were the first two things she mentioned. She went on to say, 'This gift in itself has helped you get through the many crises that you have had to endure, as your life has been a roller-coaster, to say the least! ... You are a born survivor,' she added. 'I couldn't argue with that statement,' I replied as I sighed wearily.

'You are so typical of your Sun sign, which is Gemini. They are regarded as the communicators of the zodiac.'

Although I was impressed by her findings, the chart itself was also very interesting. I found a lot of truth in the chart, particularly the marked years that pinpointed certain events. Although I did find it surprising, I do without doubt believe that every second of our lives is

mapped out by God. All our experiences, good and bad, are meant to happen, each one a learning curve.
These experiences help to nurture and develop our souls to earn us, eventually, a place in the 'Realms of Spirit'. Everything that happens has perfect timing. There is always a divine purpose to what we experience, as it is God who holds the 'blueprint'.

Mediums are 'channels' through which people can receive messages that heal. We give words of comfort in relaying messages from loved ones in the Spirit World, reassuring the loved ones here that all is well with them. These can be messages of guidance, advice and help, but most of all the fundamental nature of these communications is confirmation of the life hereafter. It gives us hope to know that at the end of our journey and in the transition of so-called 'death' we are reunited with our loved ones in the Realms of Spirit.

My gift is something I have had to come to terms with as my life's influences and experiences sculpted my pathway. It has been a metamorphosis that has led me to do the work I do today. For I know now I have found my soul's true purpose.

'Medium' is just one of the labels people have placed on me. I regard myself as someone who has been given a gift that enables me to see to see, hear and feel Spirit and the people of the Spirit World. It is a gift of communication from God.

It appears that even my name was inspired when it was given, as choosing a name for a child sometimes holds more significance than we think. Somebody in my family must have been totally inspired to name me Angela, the meaning being 'messenger' which turned out to be quite fitting.

My childhood was certainly not the 'norm'. I was brought up in a Liverpool family of Irish-Catholic descent, and we endured many turbulent times. A belief in God, the angels and all the saints, combined with a unique, warm sense of humour – the sort that only Liverpudlians tend to possess – was all part and parcel of our daily survival. Religion and humour, not only in our darkest times, were our coping techniques – and still are!

During the formative years between the ages of one and five, I and my brothers and sisters spent time in and out of children's convent homes, due to the disruption caused by my father's erratic and violent behaviour (and its effect on all of us, and particularly on my mother's health). I vividly remember one particular convent home, a place which was aptly named after the Archangel Gabriel (the Messenger): St Gabriel's in Woolton, Liverpool. It was there that I learned to kneel and pray at a much younger age than most. I also learned about my first Angel.

It was during those times that I would often be visited in my dreams by two particular nuns. At first I understood them to be a reflection of what was surrounding me. One dream was remarkably prophetic. I dreamt that one of the nuns spoke to me. She gave me a profound message that didn't make sense until it unfolded decades later. She said, 'You will grow up and tell the world about the Spirit.' I did not understand what she meant at the time, but, believe me, those words haunted me for many, many years.

The nuns continued to visit me on occasion, and still do. They were two notable 'ladies of the cloth' who have since introduced themselves to me, and I am now aware that they are actually my Spirit Guides. Together with the memories of that convent home, they became etched deep into my subconscious, along with the memories of that unfortunate period of my life.

My mother was left to raise the seven of us singlehanded, so you can imagine times were extremely difficult. As a result of my father's ongoing alcoholism and violence we – my mother and the seven of us children – had to leave our beloved Liverpool and move to a secret address in the Midlands for our own safety and protection. We moved to a small village outside Birmingham. Knowing no one, all we had was each other. It was difficult enough living in a community where you were the only Catholic family in the street. It also didn't help living with the stigma of coming from a single-parent family, let alone a Catholic family where the parents had divorced. Back then, this was religiously and socially unacceptable.

An added pressure for me personally during that time was the 'gift' that ran parallel to my turbulent world. I felt ostracized – maybe because of the circumstances, but also because of the interruptions of the Spirit World. It has always made me feel very different from other people. I, like most children, just wanted to fit in, to be like everyone else. The gift made me feel distant, even from close members of my own family, as I realized in the early years hardly anyone spoke of any experiences of a 'Spirit World' kind. I felt very alienated.

As a child I was infamous for my screaming temper tantrums, the cause of which I did not fully understand! I suppose part of it stemmed from the pure frustration of not being able to comprehend what was really happening to me. It was a combination of daily events and the interruptions from the Spirit World, which, I now believe, contributed to my tantrums.

At primary school I was described as a highly sensitive and imaginative child, who would often talk about her dreams and on occasion would be reprimanded for daydreaming and talking too much. The 'gift' at that time, I felt, was a hindrance. Little did the teacher know that, when she was telling me off for daydreaming or telling me to be quiet for the umpteenth time, she would, more often than not, be interrupting a 'Spirit communication'. I would be quite happily chattering away, playing with my little Spirit friends, the children of the Spirit World. I would be too engrossed to notice the teacher calling for my attention. This would on a number of occasions get me into a lot of trouble. I soon learned to ignore my little Spirit friends at school, as otherwise, as a result of talking to them, I would often be punished with the ruler!

I have always been sensitive. I regard sensitivity a required quality for being a 'channel', and mediums

Little Angela

are often referred to as 'sensitives'. I was so sensitive that when other children were being told off or being punished at school I would sense their fear and feel their pain, and would often end up crying with them. It was a case of true empathy. It is that level of sensitivity we need to enable us to sense the Spirit World.

Sensitivity may be regarded by some as a weakness, but it turned out to be my strength. It was not only my playtimes that were being interrupted by spirits. I would receive more visitations in my dreams. This has always been the case, and still is. For I am a 'channel' and I never know where or when I am going to 'receive'.

I realize now that, during my childhood, prophetic dreams were becoming apparent. If I'd had a vivid dream that in some way disturbed my sleep, I would wake up the next morning with vivid recollections and a compelling feeling to tell someone. Whatever I told them, it would then take place in the days that followed. The dream would soon become a reality. I would quite happily, and without question, pass on what I had received to whomever I felt drawn to tell, explaining to them what I had heard and seen within my dreams. Maybe it was because of my age and naïveté, but I just accepted all this as real. The fact that I was brought up on the mysteries of God gave me that something to which I could liken my experiences. That, and cartoons sometimes!

It seemed back then that I was in my own little world at times. The Spirit World. I must have been like a sponge, soaking up the 'energies'. I remember once tugging at my mother's dress till I was red in the face, trying to tell her that I'd seen Mr Venables, a neighbour, being taken away in an ambulance. She told me not to be silly, as she had just spoken to him. Sure enough, the next day Mr Venables collapsed and died and was taken away in an ambulance. My mother, silent, just patted me on the head. That was the only recognition of my 'gift' that I would receive as a child – the occasional pat on the head from my mother! She would also often tell me how I was getting more like my grandmother each day. I did not fully understand this remark at the time, but later learned more about the woman she was referring to: my father's mother, Kathleen Murphy.

Kathleen Murphy was a small, warm, glamorous woman, never without lipstick and beads. She loved to dance and sing any chance she got, as in her youth she had belonged to a dance troupe touring music halls and theatres. She was very theatrical. She had a fine, fiery temper and wit that no man dared wrestle with. At times she became our salvation, when she would come and rescue us and take us away for the weekends, away from all the turmoil. Her home was our fortress. It was a hive of activity, with visitors calling almost daily. People could tell the family resemblance between her and me – people said it was like looking in a mirror. Sadly, I didn't get to know her for long because of us moving away and her untimely death. But what a character she was!

It was some years later I found out that she was renowned for having a 'gift' – hence all the visitors to her house. It all made perfect sense! Her gift was that she, too, was able to see, hear and feel those people of the Spirit World. It was a comfort in itself knowing that I was not the only one, thank God!

Little did I know at the time that, when my grandmother Kathleen Murphy passed over, she and other loved ones of mine would have a future role to play in the coming years, visiting me and relaying messages pearls of wisdom from the Other Side.

I now know that those childhood memories were all very real. And, in all honesty, looking back I can say that those playtimes and dreams are my earliest recollections of Spirit World encounters.

There was a very good reason to decide to keep these spiritual experiences secret, as I eventually made a conscious decision to do. I thought it was in my best interests to dismiss the Spirit World encounters, as they continued to run parallel to my world, intermittently interrupting my growing up. It was because of that and the difficulties in my childhood that these Spirit experiences would remain hidden. I did not fully comprehend what was happening to me and I doubted that other people would understand, either. After all, I'd never asked for this 'gift'!

The experiences and lessons of my younger years were the foundations needed to develop and sensitize my soul to enable me to progress to do the work that I do now, even to the level of being able to help in cases such as murder. The results of these cases never cease to amaze me and always leave me feeling humbled. Spiritually speaking, everything that has gone before has given me the tools for what I do now.

I didn't consciously one day say, 'I want to be a "medium".' It was a case of having to surrender to it. Messages came too fast, too furious and too often for me to ignore. I had no choice in the matter, as life has led me this way. It was inevitable that eventually I would have to surrender to God's divine plan. What sticks in my mind is an old saying: 'Man plans and God laughs.' There is 'greater picture' for us all, ready to unfold along life's journey. Sometimes our early experiences are connected to what unfolds later, and some of my childhood encounters bear a connection with incidents later on in my life. Recurring coincidences, synchronicities, a pattern that is all part and parcel of God's little miracles – my life is full of them. Some people would say that it's uncanny, but I now know it isn't. I do not question anything 'strange', as my life has been extraordinary to say the least! I regard myself as an ordinary woman who has had an extraordinary life. Who has an 'extra' ordinary gift. Who lives in a mysterious world!

Grandmother's Visit

I was 10 years old when I realized something exceptional was happening. It was a November evening; I was tucked up in bed and finding it very difficult to sleep. My stomach was churning and I was feeling totally restless. I couldn't find any reason why I was feeling that way, I just knew something was going to happen. My 'psyche', something inside, was telling me.

It wasn't long after being tucked up in bed when the room was lit up by the headlights of a car pulling up outside. A loud knock came on the front door. I sneaked out of bed and crept along the landing at the top of the stairs. In the reflection of the hall mirror I could see two policemen talking to my mother. I heard one of them say that they had received a telephone call at the police station from a relative of ours in Liverpool, who wanted to pass a message on to us. The policeman said he was very sorry to tell her that Kathleen Murphy had passed away earlier that evening. I heard my mother gasp. I decided to get back into bed as quickly as possible before my mother noticed me. I knew I would be scolded for listening in to what was a serious matter.

As I lay in my bed, the policeman's words kept going through my mind. 'My grandmother is dead!' I said to myself. 'My grandmother is dead!' I couldn't believe what I had just heard. I tried to convince myself that I must have heard wrong.

With the anguish of these thoughts, I eventually fell asleep. Then suddenly my eyes opened. There at the foot of my bed my grandmother Kathleen Murphy was standing.

She was surrounded by a hazy ball of light. I kept rubbing my eyes. I took a second look. She was smiling at me. She certainly did not look dead to me! Then suddenly a beautiful feeling passed through my body. The only way to describe it is one of sheer peace and tranquillity, a feeling of euphoria. It was a feeling that went through my whole body and cleansed away all my pent-up fears and emotions. This Spirit visit was different from others I'd experienced, as it was from someone I knew and loved. She stood there smiling at me for what seemed a long time. I found myself whispering to her, 'You're not dead! You're not dead!'

She looked at me knowingly and said, 'Yes, you're right. I'm not dead. I'm all right. I'm OK, so don't you worry about me! I'll have to go now, but I will be back to see you later.' She waved and turned away as the vision faded, and with those words she disappeared, leaving me with a contented feeling as I fell back to sleep.

I woke up the next morning and my mother broke the news of my grandmother's death to me. It didn't move me in any way whatsoever. I looked at her blankly. I remembered my visit from my grandmother the night before, and with those thoughts I walked away in silence and went outside and played contentedly. I wanted to tell my mother but I couldn't, as I wanted to keep the cherished experience to myself. It felt like I'd just discovered gold and I wanted to treasure it. It was my secret knowing that my grandmother was still alive in some way, and there was no doubt in my heart that she had gone to Heaven.

Teen Years

My teenage years were full of surprises. I was getting a reputation at school for being a bit of a 'character'. Some people would say I was 'strange' because I intuitively knew things. I would make statements about people and find out later that what I had said about them was true. The word 'psychic' was never mentioned. The statements I made, I would often dismiss by making a joke of it, as I did not want to be too different. No child does. I discovered I was very good at finding things, too. If I was in earshot of anyone and heard that they had misplaced their bags or belongings, up would flash a picture in my mind of their whereabouts. I was then able to tell them exactly where they could find it.

One teacher caught me in the middle of telling someone where they would find their bag. The teacher knew full well, that I had not been in the area where I said it would be found. When my classmate returned waving it in her hand, the puzzled teacher dismissed it by saying, 'Oh, you must have a photographic memory of some sort!' He said it with a puzzled look on his face, though! I just smiled and accepted his summing up. Again, I never questioned it. It was part of who I was.

Like any other ordinary teenage girl, I was too busy discovering my own individuality to make my 'ability' an issue. I was dealing with being bullied at school for being too thin. Because of that, I learned to laugh at myself and to hide my underlying feelings. Humour was good armour at times. I thought if it ever came out about my strange 'happenings', I would be ridiculed even more.

One of my favourite subjects at school was Religious Education. Being a Catholic school, this was a prominent subject. I felt comfortable with the idea that I could sometimes relate my 'gift' to the biblical stories that we studied daily. One story that made its mark was the one about the seventh child being anointed with a 'gift'. But this was the 1970s – not biblical times! Another reason to keep quiet about my 'gift', I suppose, was the fact that it just wasn't 'trendy' enough to mention!

The one important event for every teenager is their first love. Mine, I shall never forget. It was in my last year at school, just before my 16th birthday, in 1974. A rumour was circulating round our village youth club that a new boy, who had just started to attend, happened to be the brother of a famous rock star, a member of
the rock group Black Sabbath. When a friend pointed him out to me, it was obvious whose brother he was. He was the image of him, with his long, flowing locks

and his handsome looks. He was unmistakably the younger brother of Ozzy Osbourne!

He did not ask me out straight away. We met at a mutual friend's party, where he made a beeline for me, introducing himself as Tony. He told me he had moved with his parents and family from Aston in Birmingham to the small village of Aldridge, where I lived at the time. There was no boasting about whose brother he was. Tony was modest. In no way was he like his 'wild' brother. He came across as quite shy and reserved. We courted on and off for the best part of a year, during which time I didn't have any expectations of hanging around with Black Sabbath! Which we didn't anyway!

At first I did not know what to expect. Tony was just a working-class lad who worked in engineering. I remember being asked back to his parents' house for Sunday tea for the first time. I thought I would arrive and see all the trademarks of having a rock star in the family, half-expecting that there would be gold discs on the wall and guitars hanging around, or some other rock memorabilia. But no, it was just an ordinary family home with a single wedding picture of John (Ozzy) and his first wife on a shelf above the television, alongside other family photographs. At that time Tony lived with his mum, dad and other brother. I found his parents were friendly enough. I always addressed them as Mr and Mrs Osbourne, as you did out of respect in those days. His father was a particularly warm character. He had a great sense of humour, which I admired. I can now see where Ozzy gets it from! I never met Tony's famous brother and it did not interest me, as Tony was my world at that time!

I left school and started college. My long-term plan, before Tony came on the scene, was that I would finish my college course and go on to work and live in London. Going to the bright lights of London seemed a greater attraction. When the time came, given the choice between Tony and London, I chose London as I felt that I was far too young for a more serious relationship! I wanted to experience different things in life!

Our paths separated, but Tony's chance meeting with a medium, and mine with a rock star's brother, left a significant connection to a future surprise. It was almost 30 years later that I would receive a totally unexpected 'vision' of Mr and Mrs Osbourne near a poignant time in Ozzy's life.

It was during my college course studying Tourism, that I met a lecturer called Carole, who was from South Africa. She told me she was a Spiritualist. It was the first time I had heard of such a thing before. I remember saying something like 'Oh, I believe in Heaven and the afterlife', comparing it to my Catholicism. In hindsight I realized that she, too, must have been mediumistic herself, as she said something that rang true many years later. She told me I had a gift and that she could see me up on a rostrum, travelling the world in my midlife. And that I would write a book. I just laughed it off at the time. But she wouldn't be the first or last Spiritualist to have graced my path and brought me a similar message.

After college I got my first job working as a hotel receptionist in the Mandeville Hotel in London's West End. The hotel belonged to one of Britain's largest hotel groups at the time, Grand Metropolitan. I lived in accommodation owned by the company and shared rooms with two other receptionists, Carole, who was from Birmingham, and Fiorella, who was an Italian girl from Dudley. She looked Italian, but spoke with a broad Black Country accent, which I found delightfully amusing. The way of life in London moved at a much faster pace than I was used to, and I enjoyed being surrounded by the many different cultures of the great cosmopolitan city. I have always had a fascination for people and life. It seemed that London and its lifestyle suited my personality and 'growth' at the time.

Grandmother's Orders

We were constantly working split shifts at the hotel. We would often be owed days off in lieu. The evening before one well-earned break was due, when I had planned to take a sightseeing tour around London the next day, I found that the Spirit World had different plans for me! It was one of those familiar nights when I was feeling totally restless. I found it hard to sleep, and realized I was beginning to sense that something was about to happen. As I wrestled with my thoughts, I became tired of trying to fathom it out and then, suddenly, a piercing light seemed to come from nowhere. It wasn't like an electric light. It seemed so intense and bright. The light, which seemed to grow larger and larger with each second, appeared to fill the room. I watched in shock for the first few seconds or so. I then realized how frightened I was; I hadn't experienced this phenomenon before. Actually, to say I was frightened was an understatement – I darted under the bedclothes in sheer terror! The fact that I was so far away from home did not help the matter and only added to my fear.

Then came some sort of relief. I heard a voice that sounded familiar. It was the voice of my deceased grandmother, Kathleen Murphy. She called my name: 'Angela, Angela.' I was still too scared to raise my head from underneath the sheets. Still aware of the bright light. I listened to what she had to say: 'You must go to Llandudno to visit your Uncle Bob.' She said it over and over again with urgency in her voice. Then she and the bright light disappeared as quickly as they'd come. But her voice seemed to continue echoing in my head for the rest of my sleep that night.

I didn't even begin to question her visit, as she had visited me before. And this time I was a bit older and much more logical in my thoughts. Questions were spinning around in my head. I found myself thinking out loud, 'Why do I have to go and see Uncle Bob?' I hadn't seen him since I was a small child. 'What if he no longer lives there? It's over 200 miles away!' These thoughts were swirling in my mind as I lay in my bed. Then a compelling feeling came over me. I knew I had to go. There were no more doubts or questions. The next morning I packed my suitcase. I was walking out of the door when Carole, my flatmate, arrived home from her night shift. 'Where are you off to with that suitcase?' she asked.

'Oh! I'm just going to Llandudno for a couple of days to see the relatives. See you when I get back,' I said hurriedly. I didn't want to explain further. I just couldn't bring myself to tell her any more. Carole seemed very surprised and said, 'You never mentioned that yesterday!'

'Oh! Didn't I? It must have slipped my mind,' I said, as I headed off out the door.

The journey was painstakingly long. The train seemed to stop at every station along the way. I didn't doubt my actions for one minute, though. After all, I was just following my dear deceased grandmother's orders. I arrived at Llandudno station at 7 p.m. It was a dark, cold January evening. I caught a taxi that dropped me off on the mountainside at the end of the terrace. I just about remembered what Uncle Bob's house used to look like, though I hadn't visited for many years. Things were about to unfold!

When I knocked on the door, it was answered by a lady I did not recognize.

'Does Bob live here?' I asked.

'Yes,' she said. As she turned and shouted, 'Bob, it's for you!' I could hear the hustle and bustle of people in the back of the house. I recognized my uncle as he came to the door – still with the same smiling, fresh-faced look I remembered from all those years before.

'Hello, Bob,' I said. 'You may not recognize me but I'm your niece Angela. Your brother Sid's daughter.'

'My God!' he said, as he held out his arms. 'Tonight of all nights!' He went on to explain it that it was his 25th wedding anniversary that day and every member of my grandmother's family was there visiting him. They were just about to leave for a party at the Promenade Hotel set for 7.30. What perfect timing, I thought! My Uncle Bob then introduced me to all my long-lost relatives. He regarded my unexpected visit at just that moment as a miracle! He stated that it was the first family get together since my grandmother's passing and, he said, it was as if I'd been sent to take her place!

When my grandfather set eyes on me, he was overcome with emotion as he remarked on how much I resembled my grandmother, his true love, Kathleen Murphy. 'For one glancing moment, I thought it was her as a young woman!' he said with tears in his eyes, as he gave me a big hug.

'Never mind, Granddad, she sent me in her place,' I said with a wink.

My unexpected visit was the topic of the evening. Many of my relatives commented on how strange it was, me turning up 'out of the blue'. They gave me my grandmother's place at the head of the table, where she would have sat as the grand matriarch of the family. They all concluded that I'd been sent to take my grandmother's place. I deeply regretted not being able to tell them what had really happened. I would have loved to have told them – particularly my grandfather – that my grandmother had actually sent me. But I didn't feel comfortable enough to disclose that to them. I was just seventeen.

The way in which Spirit communicated to me in this particular instance would be repeated to me time and again in the future. I almost get a feeling of detachment as I work on such a high vibration. I have learned to trust in God and the Spirit World wholeheartedly to allow them to use me as their instrument and guide me for their purpose.

Madeleine's Macca Madness

Madeleine was a young American girl from New Jersey, whom I met during a couple of lively years when I was living in Maida Vale, London, and striving for my independence. One cold February afternoon in 1976 I had just arrived back from work when the door bell rang. When I answered it, there stood a petite young woman with long straggly hair, who happened to be looking for somewhere to stay. I explained to her that the accommodation was owned by the company I worked for, and only housed employees! I found her to be very pleasant as she chatted away, explaining her visit to England. She told me she was an avid fan of the Beatles (which was an understatement!) and that she spent all her days seeking out all the old Beatles' haunts! She went on to say she had already visited Liverpool and the houses where each of the Beatles used to live. I told her that I came from Liverpool originally and had nostalgic memories of Beatlemania. She told me that Paul McCartney was recording a new album at that time, and that the Abbey Road Studios weren't too far away, and that Paul himself lived around the corner from the studios in Cavendish Avenue, St John's Wood. She pulled photographs out of her handbag of herself and Paul, whom she had met that week at the Studios. At that point I interrupted her and said, 'Isn't it strange? A few months ago I met his two aunties. They had booked in at the hotel where I work in Mandeville Place!' Prior to their visit, the hotel had received a telex informing us that all expenses incurred by the two ladies were being paid for by McCartney Productions Ltd. The telex had been sent by a secretary of Paul and Linda McCartney. I thought that was exciting enough! I'd kept a copy of the telex message as a souvenir!

When Paul's aunties had arrived at the hotel, one of them was a bit flustered as she had left her coat in the taxi. I helped her by making a string of phone calls to retrieve the coat. In return she gave me a promotional picture of Paul and Linda – she seemed so proud. She told me that Paul was away in Australia at that time and, as she had not been well, Paul had kindly paid for her to see a Harley Street specialist! Hence her visit to London. She thanked me for returning her coat and insisted I join them for a cup of tea later. This offer I had to refuse as I was not allowed to fraternize with the guests. But to tell the truth I did find a quiet five minutes to have a tea break and a chat with them. They were delightful and I found them to be two very friendly, warm-hearted people, two very down-to-earth ladies just typical of Liverpool people. It registered in later years that one of them was the famous 'Auntie Gin' mentioned in the Wings' song 'Let Them In'.

Madeleine suggested that if I wasn't doing anything the next day we could meet up and she would take me to meet Paul McCartney. It just so happened that the very next day was my day off. We arranged to meet each other at 5 p.m. She said she would call and collect me. I remember pinching myself as I shut the door on her and thinking was this girl for real, was I really going to meet Paul McCartney? Would she really turn up the next day? 'Oh well!' I said. 'We'll see!'

Shortly afterwards, my flatmates returned from their long shifts at work, telling me about all the goings-on that day. It was near bedtime when I suddenly remembered my news, and I said quite casually to my flatmate Carole, 'Oh, by the way, I am going to meet Paul McCartney tomorrow.'

'Yeah!' said Carole, unbelieving. 'And I'm the Pope of Rome!'

'Yes, honestly Carole!' I said, trying to explain. 'I have just met an American girl who is going to introduce me to him tomorrow.'

I went on to explain about the meeting with Madeleine.

'Why didn't you tell me this, when I first came in? It's not every day you get to meet THE Paul McCartney!' Carole said.

I could tell she still didn't believe me. 'Oh well!' I said, 'You'll see!'

Five o'clock the next day eventually came and Madeleine arrived just as she'd said she would. As we walked from Maida Vale to Cavendish Avenue, I became more anxious with each step, wondering how I would introduce myself and what words I would choose to say to someone *so* famous, and what we would talk about. I decided I was going to tell him about meeting his two aunties. As we reached Abbey Road Studios, Madeleine recognized one of the McCartney cars and said, 'Oh! They're here! There's "Lin's Min", as Paul calls it!' She was referring to a pink customized Mini Cooper, parked in front of the Studios. 'All we have to do now is wait a while,' she said.

While we were waiting we were joined by three other young women, who were also 'in the know' about McCartney's whereabouts! They seemed to know Madeleine. One was a Welsh girl called Kathy, another was a Cockney girl called Sheila and there was also a Dutch lady whose name escapes me! We stood for a couple of hours chatting away, sharing Beatles memories with each other. It was clear that the girls had been waiting there on a daily basis, and that this was how they spent their time! They were what I call fanatical.

It wasn't long before two figures appeared on the steps of the Studios. It was Paul and Linda! Paul shouted over, 'You lot must be cold!' referring to the bitter February weather. Paul made a beeline towards us. Pieces of paper and photographs were thrust under his nose, each girl pleading for an autograph and then asking him to pose for photographs. Paul glanced around at our small group and realized I was an unfamiliar face. He then said in a friendly way as he signed autographs, 'Hello, what's your name? I haven't seen you here before! Where do you come from?'

'Angela,' I said nervously. 'I come from Liverpool!'

'No greater place to come from, eh?' he quipped.

I quickly, though nervously, interrupted him because I knew he would probably not stay too long. 'By the way, Paul, I met your Auntie Gin. In fact, I met your two aunties,' I said, trying to capture his attention.

'Yeah? Oh really?' he said, looking surprised and interested. I explained about their stay at the hotel where I worked.

Paul clowned around for a bit, doing poses and funny faces, 'playing up' to our cameras. Linda stood back while he performed his antics. Then both of them kindly posed together for more pictures. I found them very warm and obliging. Paul was everything I expected him to be – a wonderful soul. They said their farewells before they zoomed off up the road in their little Mini Cooper.

I was left feeling dazed. I could not believe I had just met a Beatle! When I returned back home to my flatmates, waving my autographs and telling them of my (soon to be developed!) photographs, I proved to the 'doubting Thomas's that I had actually met Paul McCartney that day!

As the weeks went by, I became more familiar with the area. I would quite often walk past the McCartney's home and Abbey Road Studios. I would go out of my way on my route to work in the hope that I would bump into them again – which I did on numerous occasions! Paul, Linda and their associates got so used to our small familiar crowd that we eventually got ourselves invited to look around the famous Abbey Road Studios!

I found Linda McCartney to be a very affectionate, expressive person. She would often greet me with a hug, and she, too, would find time to pose for photographs. Some people wouldn't have expected her to behave like this, considering half the world's women wanted a piece of her husband! I always admired her and her work campaigning for animal rights. I hold a lot of respect for her morals and values, as a mother and a campaigner. Linda was a beautiful soul.

London may have been the first place we met, but it was not the last. It was 'planned' that our two souls would meet yet again. After receiving a premonition of her death, I later met up with Linda, but this time in the Realms of Spirit during a near-death experience I had in 1998. There was no doubt our souls' pathways had met and crossed for a purpose. I was touched to think that Linda had come to me for my help, in relaying her message of love …

Mothers Intuition

Mothers are more knowing than what we think. A mother can sense things about her children, more so than their male counterparts. This can sometimes be referred to as 'mother's intuition'. It is because we are not just physically attached to our children, we are *psychically* linked to them. There is a definite spiritual attachment.

Children, I believe, are Heaven-sent. They are the souls that are born and sent with perfect timing to share and touch our pathways, for whatever length of time the soul chooses. They have chosen their parents and pathways. So it may not surprise you when I tell you I predicted the sex of each of my own children. A spirit didn't tell me in any profound message, it was my own psyche, my soul, that told me. Deep down inside, I knew. Intuitively – just the same way I got to know many other things in life.

I was so confident and comfortable with the thoughts and feelings inside me that I just knew when I was expecting my second child that I was expecting a girl. So, before the baby was born, I went out and bought a first set of clothes in pink. I also booked to have a home birth, as I 'sensed' the baby was going to arrive quickly, before there would be time to get to hospital.

The morning of 6th August soon came. It was the expected date of delivery. I went into labour and the midwife arrived, well-equipped, at 8 a.m. sharp. I told her the contractions were coming every few minutes. She unpacked her equipment and prepared herself for the birth. She double-checked I had everything prepared for the new arrival. The last thing she checked was the baby clothes. When she pulled open the dressing table drawer, she stood back, aghast. She turned to me and frowned. 'Well, really, Angela, you shouldn't do this! What on earth made you buy everything pink?' she scolded. 'Who says it's a girl?'

'I do,' I said, 'and she'll be here quicker than you think!' I didn't go into any detail how I knew; I told her I'd just got a strong feeling.

Shortly after that the midwife's face was a picture! My daughter was born very quickly, within half an hour of the midwife's arrival, and was soon dressed in her pink clothes. The midwife left that morning summing it up as a case of pure luck, and saying that I had been very lucky in more ways than one that morning, having had my baby girl and having booked a home birth, as I would not have made the journey to hospital if I had booked a hospital birth.

When my children were little, I would often have premonitions about their periods of ill-health and minor accidents. I learned that, although I knew things were *going* to happen, as much as I tried to I could not *prevent* them from happening. I always had a tendency to keep these sorts of premonitions to myself, as I thought that if I mentioned them it would perhaps have some kind of sway in making them happen. Although I knew that really wasn't the case.

My total compulsion to do and say things without prior thought, which would result in profound messages being passed on to whoever was the chosen recipient, was becoming very noticeable among my family and friends. It seemed messages would come almost at the speed of light. Relaying messages would become a regular occurrence, although to me it was nothing new, as the underlying trait had always been there.

There was one personal message that had a very good reason to be 'channelled' through another medium – the reason being that I would not have wanted to accept the words that were said. I would have tried to dismiss it in some way, if it had been channelled through me. Although I did try to dismiss the message initially, it was inevitable that the words would soon become a reality.

It was a message from my late grandfather, Jack Gavin. Jack was a small man, a heroic figure. He had fought in

Grandfather Jack Gavin

two World Wars and spent almost 26 years in the RAF, but his true passion in life was football. Wherever he had travelled, he seemed to establish a football team – that is, if he wasn't playing for one! He did play professionally at one point in his career, for Wrexham in the late 1940s and 1950s, and he later became Chairman of 4th division Workington FC. One of his proudest moments was when he played against his beloved Liverpool at Anfield in 1945. He kept the programme from that particular match as a trophy, which he passed on to me before he died. The programme takes pride of place in my home and is cherished to this day. He only graced my pathway for such a short time, as I only really got to know him and to know about his heroic adventures in his final two years, when he came to live with my mother and family due to his ill-health. He passed over in 1975.

One of the first messages from Jack happened to be one of the greatest messages of hope that I've ever been given. It was a message of hope that I needed at the time, and it kept me going through one of the most difficult times of my life. It was when my youngest was just five years old. I was going through a very difficult divorce, trying to escape from the clutches of a controlling and aggressive man. To say that I was a 'victim' of domestic violence is not true. For I am a survivor. With God's strength I finally dealt with my disastrous marriage. In the process, and as a consequence, I lost everything I owned and had worked hard for. Of course, whatever I lost materially came back to me later, ten-fold. But the

PRICE—ONE PENNY.

LIVERPOOL F.C.
Official Programme

The only Official Programme issued by the authority of
THE LIVERPOOL FOOTBALL CLUB CO., LTD.

Directors:
W. H. McCONNELL, Esq. (Chairman); S. R. WILLIAMS, Esq., O.C. (Vice-Chairman);
W. H. CARTWRIGHT, Esq.; W. HARVEY WEBB, Esq.; J. H. TROOP, Esq.;
W. J. HARROP, Esq., C.C.; R. L. MARTINDALE, Esq.; G. A. RICHARDS, Esq., J.P.;
Alderman B. K. MILNE, M.C.; GEORGE KAY (Manager).

FOOTBALL LEAGUE MATCH.

LIVERPOOL v. WREXHAM

AT ANFIELD. SATURDAY, OCTOBER 7th, 1944.
KICK-OFF 3 p.m.

Right   LIVERPOOL (Red Jerseys)   Left
                                       Kemp (1)
                    Jones (2)   Gulliver (3)
               Taylor (4)   Hughes (5)   Pilling (6)
        Eastham (7)   Dix (8)   Balmer (9)   Welsh (10)   Campbell (11)

        Rogers (11) Livingstone (10) Revell (9) Bremner (8) Hancocks (7)
               Gavin (6)   Tudor (5)   Fuller (4)
                    Jefferson (3)   Jones (2)
                                     Whitelaw (1)
Left   WREXHAM   Right

Referee: Mr. J. Lawless (Bury).
Linesmen: Messrs. H. Morrell (Sale) and J. E. Thomason (Chester).

COME AND SEE THE UNDEFEATED "YOUNGSTERS" AND
LEAGUE LEADERS.
LIVERPOOL COUNTY COMBINATION.

LIVERPOOL RES. v. NAPIERS
SATURDAY, OCTOBER 14th, 1944.   KICK-OFF 3 p.m.
Admission 6d.; Boys 3d.; Stands 9d. (including Tax).

greatest reward I gained from the experience was peace of mind.

I was left with three small children to look after. I just had to pick up the pieces. At the time I was working in a nursing home for the elderly and terminally ill. This was a place where I would often witness spirits of loved ones arriving at relative's bedsides, as they came to greet and help their loved one cross over to the Other Side. I found it wasn't unusual for nurses to talk of 'strange' happenings, which was not surprising, as we all worked on the 'edge of life', walking along the fine line between the two worlds. I found that hospital environments and such-like are full of Spirit energy. I worked in that atmosphere for eight years nursing the elderly.

I had plans to re-educate myself and to build a better life for my children and myself. It was during those difficult times, struggling as a single parent, that I met a young mother called Lorraine, whose daughter went to the same school as my children. She had moved recently to the area. She was originally from Yorkshire, but had spent some years living in Germany with her husband, whom she had now divorced.

We found we had a lot in common. We were both philosophical about life as our 'cups' were always 'half full'. Our thoughts were that there were always people far worse off than us. We laughed a lot together as we shared a similar sense of humour. Not that we had a lot to laugh about! Her friendship was certainly a 'chink of light' in my life. She was obviously sent on my pathway for that reason, but there was also another, greater reason.

Lorraine called me one evening and sounded concerned. She kept asking me if everything was OK. I knew this was leading up to something else. She went on to explain that she had been to visit her mother, who lived up in Yorkshire, and while she was there her mother had been to her local Spiritualist church and had received a message through the visiting medium for someone called Angela, from someone in Spirit called Jack. Her mother was convinced it was for me, because I was the only person she knew at the time named Angela. Lorraine reluctantly began to tell me the message, but first she asked, 'Who's Jack?'

'It's my grandfather,' I said.

'Please don't be alarmed when I say this, but the message from your grandfather was that you are going to be seriously ill. But don't worry,' she emphasized, 'you will receive healing from the Other Side.'

Lorraine became aware of my continued silence as I tried to absorb the words. Words I didn't want to hear. I just hoped she was wrong. Trying to dismiss what she'd said, I replied, 'I'm OK, though. There's nothing wrong with me. I feel fine. I'm as fit as a fiddle apart from feeling a little rough round the edges from being emotionally battered and bruised.'

'Well,' Lorraine said, 'at least if you are going to be ill, you will know that you're going to be cured. How hopeful is that?'

'We'll see,' I said, 'but I just hope you are wrong. I don't think I could go through much more.' I sighed. The conversation was soon back on its usual track, as we made light of our daily endeavours with our usual humour. My grandfather's message was left engraved in my subconscious.

It was 18 months later that I was diagnosed with cervical cancer. It dawned on me then that the first part of Grandfather's message had begun to ring true. I was in a turmoil of raw emotion for a while, but no amount of crying or worry was going to change things. My greatest fear was the thought of leaving my children alone and motherless. It was soul-destroying. I had to pull myself together. I had to be strong for the sake of my children and carry on. I went on auto-pilot for a long while, functioning numbly through my daily chores. The bottom line was that it was just something else in life I had to deal with. I could have easily been angry with God. I had never felt so alone, but it was my belief in God and faith in the Spirit World, accompanied by the words of hope in my grandfather's message, that helped to keep me going. After all, I was going to 'receive healing from the Other Side', so Grandfather had said.

His message would battle through to the forefront of my mind in times of great insecurity. I tried to take from it the reassurance I needed. But fears still placed doubt in my mind as much as I believed and had faith. I had never prayed so much before in my life. In fact, I asked everybody I knew to pray for me regardless of what religion they belonged to. I was brought up with a belief in the power of prayer, and had already been a witness to God's miracles.

My insecurities would often get the better of me, however. I was like a small child at times, stamping my feet and demanding straightforward answers from God and the Spirit World. I was wanting reassurance over and over again. I realized my emotions were putting up barriers to Spirit. I wasn't getting any answers, so I thought. So I spent some time 'running' between the two churches – the Catholic one, where I would pray almost endlessly, and the Spiritualist one, in the hope that I would receive another profound message. But what I was really wanting was something 'written in stone' to say that I was going to be OK.

There were many reflective moods that I went through. I felt the need to go back to my roots and examine my life with a soul-searching visit to Liverpool. My intention was to visit all the houses and convent homes where I had lived and to speak to relatives, neighbours and friends, in order to make some sense of it all.

A few weeks before my planned visit to Liverpool, on a morning when I was driving past my local cemetery, I realized it had been some years since I had visited my grandfather's grave. In fact, I hadn't been there since the day of his funeral. Now, suddenly, the need to be physically close to his remains was overwhelming. Besides, I needed a focal point to talk to, as I had a favour to ask of him. I soon found there was no need to ask, as I was given my answer almost immediately. As I approached his grave, I noticed something lying on top of it. It was a single white artificial flower. At first, my understanding was that there had been a storm and the wind had blown it there somehow. As I bent down to pick it up, however, I heard my grandfather's voice say, 'This is for you.'

I felt overwhelmed. This flower wasn't lying there by chance. It was an 'apport' from Spirit – a present from my grandfather. My grandfather was not only giving me a flower but a sign. I clutched it in my hand and held it tight – I didn't want to lose this precious gift. I was in no doubt that it was a real sign. It gave me the answer I needed. I felt peaceful for a while. I took the flower and placed it in the grid on the dashboard of my car, as a constant reminder of my own belief and faith – but, most of all, of my grandfather's words. I just knew I was going to be all right.

It was a couple of weeks later when my friend Lorraine and I made my planned visit to Liverpool. I was driving along, heading for the city, when the traffic was diverted and I somehow got lost. I found myself parked up outside a cemetery while I was looking up my whereabouts in the *A to Z*. It dawned on me that my grandmother Kathleen Murphy was buried there. This was no coincidence – I just had to see if I could find her grave. Lorraine pointed out that I could be there all day looking at the vast number of headstones.

Lorraine was persuaded by the rain to stop in the car. As I got out of the car and into the pelting rain, she shouted, 'You must be mad. You'll be here all day. You're going to get soaking wet!'

I ignored her as I was feeling totally 'drawn' to follow a path which led from the right-hand side of the church. I meandered through the headstones and within minutes I was led to Kathleen's grave – and there was a greater surprise waiting for me. For there, sitting on her grave, was a white artificial flower, a replica of the one I had been 'given' weeks before down in the Midlands.

I was so elated. I ran back to the car almost hurdling over the headstones, with tears and rain running down my face, clutching a small white flower. I must have looked a sight! I couldn't wait to show Lorraine. I couldn't get my words out quickly enough to explain to her why I was so ecstatic. I now had, not one, but two, apports from Spirit. One from my grandfather, the other from my grandmother, both representing and saying the same – that I would be healed from the Other Side. Which I eventually was, and each day I thank God.

I now know, and believe, that every second in our lives is mapped out. This is why, when I am asked about terrible events that have happened to me, and people question me saying, 'Why didn't you see that coming?' that I can say that there have clearly been traumas in my life about which I haven't had any premonitions. It seems there are things we need to know and some things which are best left unknown. There is always a reason or a purpose why we should know, or should not know, certain things. Mediums don't claim to know everything; we can only give what we receive, and there are certain things which are sometimes best left unsaid.

There is great responsibility which goes hand in hand with the gift of Spirit. It is not about trying to be all powerful and it is certainly not about frightening people. I am an instrument of God and I have been given a gift by God, a gift that needs to be embraced, respected and nurtured. There is a responsibility not to abuse this gift in any shape or form. A belief in God is paramount. Mediums must always pray to God before we commence work of a spiritual nature, asking for help and guidance to deliver His works appropriately, enabling us to help others and Spirit.

There was no greater responsibility placed on me than when a middle-aged woman called Ruby came to visit me for a sitting one day. Almost immediately as she sat down I began to realize her troubles, as a thought came to me at the speed of light and I found myself asking her, 'Who has had trouble with her left breast?'

'I have,' she said. 'I have cancer and I am amazed how you have picked up on that straight away – which brings me to the point. I am going to be straight with you. The reason for me coming to see you today is I want to know how long I have got to live.'

I could see the look of desperation on her face. This lady needed to know not something that I couldn't necessarily answer but something that would help her. She needed some kind of comfort. I asked God for guidance and went into deep thought. I sat silent for a while and then said, 'My love. You are a woman of great faith, aren't you?'

'Yes,' she answered.

'The reason I knew about your condition instantly is that not only do I know but God knows what you are going through, too.' I went on to explain, 'I hope you understand, but I am not prepared to give you an answer, as I am not prepared to "play God" with your life. There are things we need to know in life and things that are best left unsaid,' I continued, 'but I can tell you that your mother and father are in the Spirit World and they walk alongside you, too.'

I could 'sense' her mother. She was a short, stocky lady who'd lived her life through her Bible. A lady who held a happy disposition in life. Her name was unusual. Her name was Precious. I told Ruby what I could sense and hear.

'My goodness! My mother's name *was* Precious,' she said, almost in disbelief.

'Your mother tells me that you have not taken all the medical advice that has been given to you?'

'Yes, that's true,' she said, surprised. 'I have had chemotherapy and I have decided not to have any radiotherapy, as the chemotherapy made me so ill. I know I'm terminal,' she explained.

Ruby's mother's spirit continued to communicate, talking about her childhood which had been spent in Jamaica. I then had a vision of a local Baptist church, which I recognized as one I had driven past a few days earlier.

'There is a little Baptist church you go to, so I believe, where a lot of prayers and healing thoughts are being sent on your behalf?'

'Yes, yes,' she said, sounding almost relieved.

'You must continue to go there,' I said.

I knew she did not have long to live. Again, I found myself saying with carefully chosen and 'instrumented' words, 'You will find that this September will be of great importance to you, as you will find out more about your condition.' September was a matter of only two months away.

Ruby reached over and held my hand, squeezed it and said, 'Thank you so very much. You are so blessed. You are also right, Angela. Bless you. I will go by the grace of God.' She stood up and hugged me and held on to me for a while.

'You will get your rewards,' she said as she left. I knew I would never see her again, not in this life. It was that September that I heard that she had passed over to Spirit. I often pass that little Baptist church, and each time I see her smiling face. Rest in peace, Ruby.

Past, Present and Future

The spirit of a friend's mother visited me one evening during what I was hoping would be a restful night's sleep. I woke up aware of a presence. There standing at my bedside was the spirit of my friend's mother, Mrs Atkins, a lovely lady who used to take me 'under her wing' at times and nurture me, as I would quite often during my early teen years spend weekends at my best friend's house. Mrs Atkins would pamper me and spoil me just the same as her daughter, Pam, her only child. So there she was standing beside my bed!

'Mrs Atkins!' I gasped. I was surprised at her unexpected visit. 'After all these years,' I thought!

She looked at me knowingly and said, 'Our Pam is in pain. Poor Pam.' I hadn't seen Pam for a few years, even though she lived quite locally to me.

I mumbled back, 'OK, Mrs Atkins. I will go and see Pam, OK?' making a quick promise so I could grab my precious sleep. I didn't mean to seem rude, but that night I needed my rest. It was as if I instantly knew the purpose of her visit, as if what she'd said had not surprised me. She wanted me to visit her Pam.

Something was obviously wrong for her to make this visit and be so concerned. Our loved ones who have passed over still care for us and are aware of what we are going through, and quite often communicate to let us know they are 'walking alongside us' through our every endeavour.

A busy two weeks passed, during which I felt a little bit guilty as I hadn't found the time to visit Pam yet. But a reminder came one morning as I sat in the car at traffic lights. A recognizable voice in my ear said, 'Our Pam's in pain.' It was Mrs Atkins giving me yet another reminder. With that I turned the car round and headed towards Pam's house, which was a couple of miles away in the other direction. For I'd had my usual compelling feeling that now was the right time. My logic should have told me that it was Friday morning and both Pam and her husband would be at work. But it seemed Spirit knew best.

As I turned into the cul-de-sac I could see both their cars sitting on the drive. The timing was perfect. I knocked on the door. Ken, Pam's husband, answered. He seemed surprised to see me standing there, as it had been at least three years since we'd last met.

'Well, well, well!' he said, awaiting some explanation for my unexpected visit.

'Hi, Ken. How's Pam?' I said eagerly.

'Come in. She's in the living room.'

As I approached the living room, I paused at the door and decided to put my head round first to surprise her. Expecting her to be sitting in a chair, I glanced down and there she was lying flat out across the floor. She looked as if she were trying to keep perfectly still. It was obvious that she was in some kind of pain.

'Hello, stranger,' she said with a warm smile.

'Ah, you poor thing,' I said sympathetically.

Pam interrupted me, 'Have you got a message for me?' She must have realized the purpose of my unexpected visit.

'Yes, Pam, it's from your mum,' I said. 'She paid me a visit on the Saturday a couple of weeks ago to tell me that you were in pain. I'm sorry I didn't visit you sooner.'

'Saturday,' she said, sounding surprised. 'That was the day I slipped a disc in my spine.' Her eyes started to glisten over with emotion as I described her mum's visit. I told her how well her mother had looked.

'Anyway, if you had visited me any sooner I may have not been here as I have been back and forward to hospital quite a lot lately,' Pam informed me.

'Well, Pam, it's just your mum's way of letting you know she's still around you and knows what you're going through.'

'That is so lovely, knowing that. I must tell my auntie as she is always saying that she "senses" my mother's presence around me. I wish I could sense and feel her myself,' she said.

I explained that sometimes when we grieve and want to see our loved ones so much, the emotions can block communication. With Pam being an only child, the bond and the angst of 'wanting' could be so emotionally great that it could be putting up barriers.

'Besides that, Pam,' I said, 'she's been too busy nurturing and looking after everyone else over there.'

Communication from Spirit will find a quiet time and place. I find that, quite often, communication will take place when all our psychic barriers are lowered, at such times as when we are falling asleep, during the dreamstate, or as we are waking up. Our loved ones will use the nearest 'channel' they can find. Maybe another person who is close to us or a member of the family who is sensitive enough, such as a child or a friend who is a medium, as in this case.

Sensitive Children

It is not unusual for children to receive communication from Spirit, as young children are often the greatest 'sensitives'. They hold no boundaries in their thoughts or expression. Sometimes they will give the greatest evidence of the Spirit World. A classic case is when we find them mentioning particular names or details of loved ones who have passed over, which we know cannot possibly be known to them. They will sometimes act out the communication during their playtimes. There is so much we can learn about the Spirit World from children. I have discovered that by having a 'channel' in the family, the gift can be passed down in such a way that the channel's presence will help to develop any sensitive child. Like me with my grandmother and me with my very own daughter.

My daughter one day did what I can only call Spirit writing, at a time when she could not read or write. She was barely four years old. I was visiting a friend called Mary, who is one of the most optimistic people you could ever meet. The only thing that got her down was where she lived. She was unhappy there and longed to move. While we were having a cup of tea and a chat, I gave my daughter some paper and a pen to keep her occupied. I said to Mary, as a thought came in from Spirit, 'You know what, Mary, you're going to be moving in August! I hear August. You're definitely moving in August,' I affirmed, as Spirit gave her the answer to her much asked question.

'I can't see that happening. It's August in a couple of weeks. I can't move that quick,' she said, dismissing it.

'Ah! But, Mary, never say "never" to Spirit. There are no clocks in the Spirit World, as there is no true sense of time. It may be next August, but you will definitely move in August,' I said, standing my ground. I was giving her the answer she had longed for, but she still had an air of scepticism about her.

Just then my little girl came over to us, holding a piece of paper in her hand. I asked her if I could have a look to see what she had drawn, but she pulled back her hand and insisted on giving Mary the piece of paper, as she said proudly, 'Mary, this is for you,' making out it was some sort of present.

Mary looked at it and jumped back as if she had been given some sort of electric shock.
'Oh my God! Look at this!' she squealed in disbelief. She couldn't believe her eyes. She passed it over to me. I looked at the picture my daughter had drawn, in the style you would expect from a four-year-old – but there, written above the picture, was a clearly legible sentence, although the words did not have spaces in between. The message read, 'Timeyououtthehouse'.

My daughter could not read or write – she was barely four years old. The only explanation is that her little hand had been guided by Spirit. We were actually looking at a classic case of Spirit writing. We looked at it over and over again, examining the whole paper. I was amazed and touched by my little girl's sensitivity.

Poor Mary seemed baffled by it. But it certainly opened her eyes. I tried to explain that there was also an interpretation to the picture my daughter had drawn underneath the sentence. She had drawn four very separate things: a block of flats (Mary's dwellings), a figure standing alone (Mary), a door and a ball of sunshine.

'Look, Mary!' I said. 'Even the picture tells a story.' Pointing, I explained, 'Look, there's your block of flats and that little figure is you, and there's your new door bringing you happiness and sunshine.'

The words and pictures had an impact on us both at the time, but it wasn't just the answer to Mary's problem, as there was something greater about to unfold. The drawing and words, we would come to see, were revealing a chapter in Mary's life that was a testing time for her, but I'm glad to say it had a happy ending.

Two weeks later, in August, while Mary was on holiday, her flat was burgled and set on fire by the culprits. Very few things were retrievable. Mary was devastated, as she lost everything she owned. The police had never known such an 'aggravated burglary'. The story made headline news in the press and on television. Mary had to move to a new home as a result of the fire. She learned about the strength of people's humanity, as she was overwhelmed by people's kindness as they gave her support and helped her to piece her home and life back together again. The experience made her more philosophical about life and more happy about her surroundings than she'd ever been.

As for my daughter's miraculous Spirit writing, wouldn't it be wonderful if that had made headline news, too? Sadly, we live in a society of too many nonbelievers, who are quick to judge and condemn. But at least it became my treasure and a tool I could use. I have since used her picture, among others, as an example of Spirit phenomena in talks and seminars in my travels around Europe. I first showed it to a group of people while delivering a talk at the Baker Foundation in Spain. While discussing the interpretation of the picture, a lady remarked that she thought the ball of sunshine may have represented fire, as it could actually be a picture of a ball of fire. I reminded her that my interpretation of the picture at the time was to give hope, not to instil anxiety.

My daughter's picture is framed and takes pride of place in my little gallery at home among other memorabilia relating to Spirit phenomena, reminding me of the physical evidence that the Spirit can produce. It's a nice thought that my daughter's picture may have had a hidden message to say, that one day she, too, will be a good medium. First, though, I wanted her to be a good Catholic. I made a conscious choice to bring up my children in the Catholic faith. I wanted to give them some foundation and concept of the understanding of God, and to show them the example of Jesus, who I believe was Himself the greatest 'channel' and healer of all, and His life and works. Most of all, I wanted them to have faith, which is a belief in the unseen, in the hope that they, too, in their own time and in their own minds, could build a greater sense of spirituality, not necessarily a sense of religion, though I believe all spirituality and all religion lead to one God, who is a God of love, light and compassion.

TIRED. IN JUNGLE THE ROCKS

Spiritualism and Me

I have known the torment of Catholic guilt, as a child and as an adult, for having this so-called 'gift'. The gift, accompanied by my beliefs, I found did not marry up with the Catholic faith. This induced turmoil and confusion within me. I would often come across people who were rather judgemental about my gift. One particular person was an old Catholic school friend whom I met again in later years. Within the first few seconds of meeting her she told me proudly she was no longer a Catholic but was now a born-again Christian.

'Good for you,' I said, 'and I suppose I'm what you'd call a Spiritualist medium now.'

Her jaw dropped. She grabbed my arm and squeezed it gently, as if I was in need of some comfort, as she very politely said, 'I know you're a lovely person, but I don't approve of you calling and chanting up these spirits. It's not good, you know.'

I quickly replied, 'My dear, I have never "chanted" or "called up" a spirit in my life. They just come to me for help in communicating messages of hope to loved ones here. I have no choice in the matter, and after all who are we to judge? Everyone to their own, eh?'

She looked awkward and the conversation soon ended with a quick goodbye.

That was the sort thing I was up against – people's prejudices and sheer ignorance.

I somehow wanted an explanation or even a blessing from the Catholic Church, as it felt important to me at the time because the struggle within me was great. I was in my early 30s when I decided to ask my local priest. He came across as a reserved, well-read man who, in my opinion, seemed to have that direct line to God – there was definitely an 'aura' or presence about him. I wanted to know his views on my 'gift', as I was at the time still attending Mass with my children, although I occasionally frequented the Spiritualist church as well. I suppose at the back of my mind I was seeking some sort of approval or acknowledgement, so my spirit could be released from the chains of confinement among the man-made rules of religion. I felt this would enable me to be free to explore fully my sense of spirituality.

It was not unusual then for the local priest to do his rounds visiting his parishioners. He would often pop in for a cup of tea and a chat. I remember plucking up the couurage one day to ask him. I initially 'instrumented' the conversation to the subject of spiritual gifts. I felt nervous, like a child in the confessional booth trying to conjure up some 'sins' to pay penance for. I asked, as if in a hypothetical way, 'What would you say about people who had visions, premonitions and visitations from loved ones who have passed over? Is that not a gift, Father?'

He looked at me over the top of his glasses, with one eyebrow raised. I sat rigid with apprehension, awaiting his response. I just knew he knew I was talking about me. He paused for what seemed the longest time, as he thought for a while, and then he said, 'Angela! Take it as a blessing, a gift from God. But be careful what you do with it!'

This statement seemed to stop the conversation for a while and I turned the subject to something less profound. I didn't dare ask him anything else, as he wasn't the most approachable person.

After this so-called 'confession' I felt relieved, for it was something I was wanting and needed to hear for a long time. I would say that it was after that poignant moment I was able to embrace my gift fully and move on. After all, I now had the Church's opinion that I had been truly blessed with a gift from God. I would have loved to have asked the priest's opinion on Spirit

Guides, as I was already aware of their existence, but I didn't dare, as his raised eyebrow spoke volumes!

I must say, more recently I have been given a blessing from a Monsignor of the Catholic Church in gratitude and recognition for my work involving Soul Rescues, when we both became involved in one of the most disturbing cases of so-called 'poltergeist' activity.

There have been many personal messages given to me by my Spirit Guides and loved ones, and some from Spiritualist mediums who have just happened to grace my pathway from time to time. The majority of the messages from Spiritualist mediums have all been with regard to my work or, shall I say, the work that I've been told I was going to do on behalf of Spirit. These messages have now all come true, as for a number of years now I have had an association with Spiritualism and given demonstrations in Spiritualist churches in the UK and Spain.

My working association with Spiritualism started about 10 years ago. I had my first – totally unexpected – invitation to share a rostrum with the president of Brownhills Excelsior Church, who had heard about me from people in the local community. It was just a coincidence – or maybe not – that one Sunday I decided at the last minute to go to church on the evening when the medium, who was scheduled to take the service, had cancelled at the last minute. As I

arrived, I was pointed out to the President by one of the congregation and was asked to join him on the rostrum. After a lot of coaxing, I somewhat reluctantly (I was petrified!) took my first stand on a rostrum and gave my first messages to the Spiritualist movement. After that, invitations began to snowball in. They came by word of mouth, eventually
covering the length and breadth of the UK, and from other Spiritualist organizations abroad, such as the Baker Foundation in Torrevieja, Spain.

Over the years I have met some wonderful people on my travels, from both sides of the 'veil', and I continue to serve the Spiritualist movement as a duty to my personal beliefs. I adhere to all the Seven Principles of Spiritualism wholeheartedly, but I also hold an added sense of spirituality, as I feel that each person's relationship with God is as unique as they are themselves.

John's Rainbow

Coincidence and synchronicities are spiritual threads of the weave which makes up the fabric of the 'tapestry of life'. Sometimes we are blessed to feel the richness of the cloth and to see the beauty in the colours that have created the picture.

Impulsiveness has always been a trait of mine, and sometimes it is ignited as a direct result of listening to and trusting my 'inner voice' without question as it steers my thoughts and actions at times. One such moment was while I was out shopping one day. I had no intention of going to a card shop. I seemed to drift casually into the shop, to find myself browsing through the cards.

I noticed a card with a rainbow on the front. I felt drawn to it. I picked it up and read the beautiful prose written on the front. It wasn't the usual greeting card but one expressing feelings to someone who was finding life difficult. I remember it ended with the words 'God cares and so do I'. With no one in mind to give it to, I felt I had to have it. I bought it and tucked it away in a drawer, keeping it for the sheer beauty of its words. Or so I thought.

The real reason I bought it unfolded a year or so later. I was on a visit to Colwyn Bay in north Wales with my Aunt Joan, who had asked me to take her to visit an old friend of hers called Cindy, whom I'd never met before. We planned to stay at Cindy's house for the weekend. When we arrived, Cindy made us both very welcome. She was a warm Northern lady who could be mistaken, by her looks, to be one of our very own family. I was quite taken by the remarkable likeness. We laughed about it. Cindy was a divorcée and mother to two grownup children. Her only son, John, was a talented dancer who had achieved his dream of dancing on stage, in a London production. Despite having a chronic illness for a number of years, he lived his life to the full, knowing that his future might not always be so bright. At that time he was appearing almost nightly with his dance troupe in the musical *The Phantom of the Opera* starring Michael Crawford in London's West End.

Cindy showed us photographs of her talented and very handsome son. She was understandably so very proud. The weekend flew by. We had enjoyed each other's company very much; we laughed at the same things and about the number of times when people had asked us whether we were related. Uncannily we found out there were many similarities between us. I concluded there was obviously a 'psychic link' going on. Our pathways were meant to converge, but for what reason? I didn't yet know.

It was when we were saying our goodbyes, as I was sat in the car ready to pull out of the drive, that Cindy was interrupted by the house phone ringing. She asked us to wait while she dashed back into the house to answer it. Cindy was gone a long time. Her absence made me feel uncomfortable. I sensed there was something wrong. We heard what we thought was the sound of Cindy crying. I got out of the car and walked back into the house to find Cindy crumpled in a chair, crying and looking pale and shocked. She told us that John had been admitted to hospital. He'd had some sort of mental breakdown and she needed to be in London as soon as possible.

As she clearly wasn't fit to drive, I suggested she travel down with me to the Midlands while she got over the initial shock; she could then travel from there to London by train.

On our journey Cindy opened up about all her fears. All I could do was listen to her heartache. I decided to take time off from work so that I could go down to London with her. After all, she was on her own like me and my heart went out to her.

I met John for the first time the next day in Ealing Hospital, in very sad circumstances. He was what you'd call a very beautiful young man. He had the type of beauty that Elvis had – classically tall, dark and handsome. He also definitely had an aura about him. He drew people to him, patients and hospital staff alike. It was obvious how much John and his mother loved one another by the way he clung to her and she to him. Mental illness is one of the cruellest diseases. It was one of the saddest things I'd ever witnessed.

John mistook me for a relative, in his confusion. Cindy and I later raised a smile about this.

During the following months, Cindy would often call in and visit me on the way to and from visiting John. If it were one of my scheduled days off, I would join her to visit him. Eventually John was transferred to a hospital in Denbigh, north Wales.

One morning, Cindy called me unexpectedly early. Her voice sounded almost robotic. It was obvious she was in total shock. She said, 'John's dead. The funeral is at 10.30 next Friday at St Thomas' Church, Rhos on Sea.' She hung up before I could get my breath back. I understood her urgency to let people know. I tried for days to call back but couldn't get through.

At one point I had to give myself a good kick, as I was questioning whether to go or not.

I realized I just had to be there to give her my support, now when she needed it most.

It was then I remembered the card with the rainbow on it. It took me some time to find it, but I was determined because now I knew whom it was meant for.

I arranged to collect my Auntie Joan in the early hours of the Friday morning, to enable us to get to Rhos on Sea for 10 a.m. Somehow on the way there, I took a wrong turning and got lost. I began to panic. I pulled up in a street in a small town, not having a clue where I was. I said to my aunt, 'We'll ask that man there where St Thomas' Church is.' I knew we couldn't be that far away. To my surprise, when we asked the man answered, 'John's funeral ...' He was obviously sent to us, with perfect timing. He continued to give us directions, saying we could make it on time to follow the cortège leaving the house.

As we turned the corner into John's street, Cindy spotted my car. She ran over to us saying, 'I knew you'd come, I knew you wouldn't let me down.'

The day had been sunshine and showers; I'd noticed several rainbows in places, even one, rather poignantly, over the house as we left, as well as one over the church and one over the cemetery.

There was a large group of people at the ceremony, which included all the members of the dance troupe John had belonged to. They had travelled up from London and paid tribute to John by wearing their soft leather dance shoes as part of their smart attire, which complemented the *Phantom of the Opera* song that was played as he was carried out to his resting place. And there, another rainbow graced the skies.

And later, back at the house, you couldn't help but notice the majestic rainbow that stretched across the sky, above the house and across into the sea.

It was then I remembered I hadn't given Cindy her card. She opened the envelope and gasped. She began to cry almost uncontrollably. Then, pulling herself together, she tried to explain. 'My John sent you to me today ... My John sent you,' she said repeatedly. She continued, 'You don't know how much this card means to me.' She asked me if I had noticed the amount of rainbows about that day. I said I had.

'That was a sign,' she said, 'from John ... and now you have given me another, a solid keepsake from John ... You do not know how much this card and rainbows mean to me ...'

Battling through her tears, she went on to explain, 'It was a few years ago. John had bought me a rainbow made out of stained glass, a sun-catcher, which I hung on my window.

'On the night that the police rang to tell me that they had found a body, the sun-catcher had fallen and smashed seconds before the call.

'And I remember the last conversation I had with John, when he told me he was having trouble sleeping. I told him to lie down and relax, to close his eyes and to think of beautiful things, to think of the colours of the rainbow ...' She cried once more. 'Now you'll understand why rainbows mean so much.' She hugged me and held on to me.

She had cried for the first time that day, and for the hours that followed she held on to my arm, as if gaining comfort knowing that I was her link to John.

The rainbows in the sky that day were a sign. They were like a spiritual stamp, sealing the love between a mother and her son.

Whenever I see rainbows I cannot help but think of John. Sometimes he communicates to me, 'showing' me a pair of soft leather dance shoes. They were first 'shown' to me when I was giving a sitting to a young man. Up flashed a clear picture of soft leather dance shoes in my mind. It triggered a memory of John and a communication. It encouraged me to say to the young man, as he was sat down waiting to begin his sitting, 'You're a dancer, aren't you?' He looked at me, taken aback. 'Yes,' he said nervously.

'Your dream is to be a dancer in a West End show,' I said. I knew my thoughts were being inspired by John. The young man then admitted that that was, indeed, his driving ambition.

I told him he would succeed, just like John. He was delighted with his message, and so was I to think that John had paid me a visit.

It was obvious that John's spirit would connect with anything relating to his love of dance. The influence of his spirit was present some time later, when my daughter had just won the East of England Championship for her Irish Dancing. A photographer insisted that the ideal background for her photograph would be the rainbow painted on a display he had just spotted in the entrance hall of the building.

On one of many visits to relatives in north Wales, I paid a short visit to Cindy, intending to stay for a quick a cup of tea and a chat. After we finished our cup of tea, she insisted I go with her to visit John's grave. I obliged.

It was my first visit to his graveside since the funeral. The stormy weather didn't deter us at all. The ground underfoot was muddy; our shoes were caked with mud. As we made our way back to the car, Cindy wiped her feet on the only bit of tissue we could find. Realizing there was no more tissue, she glanced over at a pile of leaves and suggested I wipe my feet there. As I did, what popped out of the leaves but a white artificial flower. Cindy looked surprised. She knew about my experience of receiving apports from Spirit and my experience of the two white artificial flowers given to me by my loved ones. I had told her about those experiences shortly after she was 'given' her rainbow card.

Now Cindy laughed and cried at the same time, saying, 'That's my John, sending you a flower.' She was obviously overwhelmed. It gave her the added comfort she needed, and me an addition to my collection of reminders of the overwhelming proof of the power of Spirit.

We can all gather signs and symbols from our loved ones, whether it is flowers or rainbows, or the very things that are personal to us. Our relationship does not end just because we have lost our loved one's physical body. It is God and His will that allows our loved ones in Spirit to communicate in many shapes and forms. After all, God moves in mysterious ways.

Balloons

Any object can play a role involving a significant 'sign' from a loved one. It is more often witnessed by the individuals making it more poignant and personnel to them alone. But when some large universal display of a 'sign', happens amongst a large group of people the impact can be immeasurable to those believers but casting a questionable eye opener topic to sceptics.

Universal happenings set with perfect timings can only be deemed as a 'miracle' to those who believe and a talking point to those non-believers during the time spent witnessing, whilst out of their comfort zone.

One such series of events was threaded, engrained and engraved with 'miracles' great and small.

It was one early evening when I took an arranged telephone call from a lady named Alison, who seemed so eager but desperate to talk or should I say 'listen'.

I 'sensed a young man in spirit wanting to interrupt my thoughts as eager and as desperate to his mother 'in waiting'.

The bond between mother and child is a natural phenomenon so they say, but it is spiritually inseparable like an invisible umbilical cord which is never severed, even in the process of death.

"Who's Michael" I said almost instantly.
"My son" she replied.
She seemed relieved just to hear his name being mentioned.
And so was I.
Michael began to 'show me' the conditions surrounding his passing in a powerful series of 'visions'. I could see a beach. It looked familiar to me.

'It was Blackpool Beach' Alison confirmed.
The familiarity I felt, confirmed to me also, as it was a place I'd visited as a small child.
Michael continued to connect with his mother as he mentioned his brothers and sister, and family, particularly his twin brother.
I told her everything seemed to happen so quickly in those 'last moments'.
Michael, although a good swimmer, seemed to get into trouble with an undercurrent. Michael knew of the grievance that his mother had towards the Coast Guards response that day, the delay or lack of duty as the case may be and the on-going legal situation too.

He knew of his twin brother's 'struggle' with the feeling of helplessness. Michael wanted to tell him in particular, that he was okay in Heaven and not to worry about him and that he knows he did everything he could possibly do that day.

"He wants him to keep remembering the laughs and the mischief they got up to" I added.

There was so much power to the love being conveyed as often is the case with children and young people who communicate.

Alison responded to each statement with a dominant but relieved 'Yes' .
She added she could hardly believe what she had heard down the phone line.
I explained there was 'no distance' or barriers as such to spirit's intervention
Michaels loving 'vibration' was high, alongside his mother's sensitivity, belief system and understanding.
The 'ingredient conditions' seemed perfect and clear
Alison then thanked me and invited me to Michaels first year Memorial service which was due to take place a few weeks later in the July' on Blackpool's Beach.
She said she'd invited the local media also as to draw attention to the on-going 'campaign' she had.
I stated that if it was at all possible I would attend but not knowing my commitments at hand I couldn't actually say.
It was during that last part of the conversation I was interrupted by Michael's spirit yet again … he wanted to continue to communicate by mentioning three things that Alison just couldn't confirm and actually dismissed them all. She said adamantly, there seemed

very little or no explanation to why Michael would mention them.
The first thing I visualized was too much of an obvious symbol. I was hesitant to express and describe what I was being 'shown', but through experience I just had to relay, what I received' no matter how obvious or strange as the case maybe.

"Michaels showing me a black hat labelled with a 'KISS ME QUICK' logo on it. (A souvenir that is synonymous to Blackpool's Pleasure Beach history)
I can hear that recent popular song being played, you know, that rather rude one. I could hear it clearly.... 'Its..'My sex is on fire' song -by the Kings of Leon. I exclaimed ... that's what it is, I said. As I began to hear the song so clearly.
I then told her he was talking about 'someone having a tattoo'?
'Erm!.No,no....no!' came, the rigid reply.
She firmly said that there was no relevance to the three things I had just mentioned.
So in my pearl of wisdom, I asked her to not to dismiss anything, as I knew exactly what I'd heard and 'seen' and quite often something which doesn't seem to be accepted into the equation at that time, apparently, always seems to fall in to place later, with or for greater purpose.

I quite confidently said to her 'Please make a note, of what I'm saying as something's have a habit of becoming known and making sense later'

'Oh okay then' she agreed.
'I look forward to meeting you one day
soon, hopefully' She said.
We said are goodbyes, but how I wished it would of all struck cords till the very end of Michael's message.
 But everything in life, even our disappointments are for greater purpose and this was such a case.
A couple of hours later I had an unexpected phone call from Alison. It seemed she couldn't get her words out quick enough. She went on to give validation of those three final 'statements' of Michael's communication, as she reeled out....
"After asking around the family, Michaels twin brother confirmed that Micheal had played a prank and had hidden a 'kiss me quick' hat in his bag, as a 'quirky' little reminder of the holiday on his return, which he didn't discover till he got home and as for the song.... Micheal had actually been singing it aloud, moments before he had entered the water and but the mystery of the 'tattoo' you mentioned took longer to unravel, but it was his younger brother that had the answer to that, after he presented me with a drawing he'd done and said 'This is it!'.... This is my very own design, it is what I want as a tattoo, when I'm old enough' he said. The tattoo commemorated Michael. She gasped.
 'Oh my God Angela! Absolutely, everything that Michael communicated was remarkably true. Your so gifted! Bless you!'
 'I find it comforting to know that Michael's okay, and still around visiting his family by the sounds of it...

Thank you, so, so, very much Angela you're amazing!" She exclaimed.

'I'm not, you know' I said. 'Its Gods loving spirit that is'.

I'm just an instrument, a messenger' I explained.

We both seem to express a big sigh of relief although for different reasons but in the wonderment of spirits 'loving embrace' all the same. I could sense her relief and solace even, if only for a while.

But more spiritual wonderment was yet to come, at Michael's First Memorial Service which I'd only made 'half a promise' to attend.

The date in July soon came round and it was by no coincidence or suprise that I had to book a meeting in Blackpool with a potential Agent, who had scheduled it on the morning of the day of Memorial. I was just meant to go it seemed.

I hadn't been able to contact Alison to let her know I was planning to attend. All I remembered was that the time of Service was 2.30 pm and that people were planning to meet on the Pier beforehand.

I left the meeting that day later than expected. Time was pressing on. I soon became aware of the sheer density of the traffic. I'd underestimated Blackpool's popularity, as I hadn't visited it for decades. Besides it was the height of the holiday season too.

I prayed for a parking space near the Pier. I saw the sign 'Central Pier', and with perfect timing one space became available a stone throw away.

I panicked a little when I realised there was more than one Pier. There was north Pier and South too.

I'd only caught on to Alison's words as the 'Pier at Blackpool' If this wasn't the one, I feared I would miss the event. I prayed for Micheal to show me where his family was. I looked up above and asked out loud. I did gain a couple of strange looks from passers by, as I pleaded desperately but I was being 'intuitively' lead as I headed for the Central Pier. Just after the outburst of my request, I spotted a young women scurrying along, heading in the same direction, carrying a cardboard box. I felt totally compelled to catch up with her, as I did, I asked her if she was going to Michael's memorial. She gave me a surprise look and told me the balloons for event was in the box she was carrying. She said she was very conscious of the time, particularly, as she was helping with arrangements.

I thought her 'timing' was just perfect.

Alison and her family greeted me warmly, although they seemed to be anxious, waiting at the end of the Pier.

Myself and Alison took a stroll and chatted. We talked about the events of Michael's last moments and the plans for the day and the paramount reason for the release of the balloons at the Beach, not only in the memory Michael but in hope that it would also draw more media coverage of his untimely death, to help highlight the legal grievance she held about Michael's passing on that fateful day.

Alison began to fret over the weather, as a storm brewed up lashings of rain, into the choppy sea below us. She stated disheartedly, that the balloons will have 'no chance' of taking flight now.

It was one of those moments in hindsight. I began to question why I should of made such a seemingly bizzare statement regarding the weather.

I grabbed her arm to reassure her and said 'Don't worry the rain will stop in time'.... I questioned my rationality... I quickly went on to talk about the gesture of 'Balloon releasing ceremonies' I had previously attended or should I say Memorials where balloons had been released, what sprung to mind, was a little 'miracle' Id witnessed whilst at a memorial service regarding Balloons. Maybe there was a purpose why I had to tell her, I thought.

I began to tell Alison of my experience. She listened attentively.

I explained, It was whilst in attendance at Liverpool Football Clubs Hillsborough Disaster 20th Anniversary Memorial Service.

On this occasion I found myself seated just behind the Media section, allocated to all the Sports Commentators and Radio Presenters. That year it was being aired 'live' nationally on BBC Radio because of the landmark Anniversary. I was in earshot of all that was being expressed and aired. The famous Kop end of the ground had been allocated as usual, to the families of the victims. The weather was unusually beautiful for the month April, a blue sky with beaming sunshine and no ounce of wind, there seemed a fittingly stillness about the ground.

The usual 'closing' of the ceremony began with the release of 96 red Balloons, each one representing a 'loved one' who died that day.

We watched them rise up vertically and then all of a sudden a totally unexpected gust of wind came and blew the balloons sideways towards the Kop end where the 'loved ones' stood. . It took me by surprise, although it confirmed my belief in 'miracles'. I did hear some sounds of a 'recognition' around me but the best thing was, that the commentator actually made reference to what he and everyone else was 'witnessing' 'live' on air, even though he thought it strange and uncanny.

My reference seemed to cheer Alison up a little, as she warmed to the significance that Michael was a fan of Liverpool football club unbeknown to me, as she said 'You were meant to tell me that'.

That what was a little miracle in itself and nothing but.

And just moments before we decided it was time to make our way to the beach, the rain actually stopped.

I thanked God for the brighter clouds that began to adorn the skies.

The family and friends gathered on the Beach. The Media arrived too. Loving words was recited and a piece of music played.

Then an even bigger gesture of love was about to happen, with the release of dozens of multi-coloured Balloons. As we stood for some time watching the winds making them drift into the skies. The balloons seem to dance and rearrange themselves. The arrangement left an impression in the skies as well as our hearts.

I then noticed something and I can't say I was the first but some people must of stared in silent disbelief for a while, as the Balloons formed a clear but significant letter 'M' as they drifted into the distance across the sky.

My reaction was to close my eyes, as I knew sometimes my mind can receive things and it can be projected onto the psychical world. But to 'seal' what we were all meant to be a witness to, it actually took the voice of a small child, a little girl, to recognise and draw everyone's attention to what was happening, talk about 'out of the mouths of babes'.,

The universal energy of Gods work was present. The little girl seemed to squeal with delight and in awe as she shouted…

"Look mommy a letter 'M' for Michael".

We all stared wide-eyed at the balloons formation in the sky with believers and non-believers aghast.

The letter 'M' for Michael was purely a Miracle of which I have no doubt.

A signed signature adorned across the heavenly skies to let us know, that all is well.

An unforgettable memory of Michael.

God Bless you.

Michael Sheehan

Sister Bridget & Sister Therese

It was just another 'visit' – or so I thought. I recognized the spirit to be that of one of two nuns who had frequented my mind in turn, periodically, over the years. I had already sensed and regarded them as my Guardian Angels or my Spirit Guides, which are one and the same. I am, and have always been, comforted knowing that I am being watched over and guided by such beings. The nun stood alone, smiling at me yet again. She had never spoken to me or even told me her name, until it dawned on me one day to ask.

I was becoming more intrigued to know the reason for her recent spate of visits. She had never paid me so many visits as she did during the time I was working as a residential social worker in a children's home. It was if she was in awe of the children. I felt her presence more than ever before. I sensed that at some time in her physical life she must have worked, like me, with children. It felt as though she was doing her best to guide me in my work, but looking back on my actions and thoughts she cast a definite influence and there was a reflection of her personality about my own persona.

One evening I had arrived home from a late shift, feeling a bit stressed and concerned about everything and everyone. As I lay in bed with the worries of the day churning over in my mind, a clear vision of her appeared as she interrupted my thoughts yet again. There she was as usual, smiling at me, inducing that peaceful feeling her presence gave me. I then gave up wondering about her and said to her, almost shouting, 'Who are you? Please tell me your name! What is your name?'

In my mind I heard a faint soft voice reply, 'Sister Bridget,' in a soft Irish accent. The vision faded. I had a name, or so I thought. I fell asleep. As I woke up next morning, however, with the name still fresh in my mind, I was feeling unsure. Did I hear her right? She had spoken so softly.

I began to question what I had heard. I wanted to know for sure that her name was Sister Bridget. I began doubting, as I knew most nuns take the name of a saint but I couldn't recall any Saint Bridget stories at school.

Confirmation came a few hours later when I had gone to visit a close friend, who had just come back from a holiday in Ireland. As usual she'd brought me back a bag of souvenir goodies. One little surprise among them was an emblem of a cross made of straw – it was a Saint Bridget's cross. My friend wondered why I was so overwhelmed by it, as she didn't know its significance. It was more than a cross. For me it was my answer.

Bridget's influence was so strong. One day in a team meeting at work, we were discussing how best to meet the needs of the children. I found myself making a point about their spiritual needs and how little these were recognized. I put a case forward stating fundamentally how equally important spiritual needs are, and I suggested that the children should be given an introduction to faith or spirituality, so that they could explore for themselves, also taking into consideration that we were serving children from many different cultures.

My suggestions went down like a lead balloon! I could see I was up for a challenge when one worker said, 'If you think you can get the children up on a Sunday morning, that in itself would be a miracle, but to get them to go to church as well would be something else!' It was then suggested that, as I had brought up the subject in the first place, I should make it *my* role to see to the children's spiritual needs!

'No worries. I would love to. Besides that, I believe in miracles!' I said with a cheeky grin on my face. I liked nothing more than a challenge!

My theory on how to coax the children was to befriend the 'ring leader' – the oldest child in the group – and the others should follow suit, in theory. Besides that, I did have a good rapport with them, or so I kept telling myself.

It was a testing time that first Sunday. As usual on a Sunday they enjoyed nothing better than to lie in their beds till late. So, I was never so proud as when I saw that each and every one of the seven children had got up. They were washed and dressed, looking like shiny new pins and eagerly waiting for me as I came on duty. One child had even made an extra effort and put on a suit jacket. Miracles do happen! We all piled into the minibus and off we went to visit our first church. It was a memorable occasion and the children, apart from being a bit nervous, actually showed that they enjoyed it. They started to ask serious questions, although they found some things to be a bit of a giggle at times. I tried to answer their questions as best I could – with the influence of Bridget beside me – and overall their behaviour and conduct was an example to others. Miracles never cease!

The children began to really enjoy their weekly visits to different churches and places of worship. One of their favourites was the Gospel church. They loved the atmosphere and, most of all, the music and singing.

A couple of the children expressed their appreciation one Sunday by eating far too much food, offered to them while visiting a Sikh temple. They later 'expressed' it all over the minibus on the way home! What happy memories, though.

I spent four years working at that particular children's home until just before its closure, when I found other employment as a family social worker in a Child Protection Unit. I was sad to leave. It saddened me more to think that the children there would have to come to terms with yet another change in their lives that they did not want or did not ask for. I left them with a reminder. As my leaving present to them, I chose to buy them a framed picture of 'The Sacred Heart' – a picture of Jesus on which I had written at the bottom, 'To my Angels with dirty faces'. Quite a fitting caption, I thought, taken from one of my all-time favourite films. The children were delighted with it – in fact they fought over where to hang it! I heard that when the children's home finally closed down the children drew straws for it, but I can imagine the biggest and the toughest child won!

Bridget's work had been extremely influential and instrumental, to say the least, and I smile when I think of her influence. If it had been any stronger, I would have converted them all to Catholicism and Irish music! Sometimes it is only by looking back that I begin to realize how inspired by her spirit I really was. My work continued in social services for another nine years, but I never felt Bridget's presence as strongly as I did in those times working in the children's home.

I moved on to work with a team of 20 social workers within a Child Protection Unit. Some of my colleagues became aware of my beliefs and my 'gift'. Some had a clear understanding, others were ignorant of the facts – but the majority seemed fascinated. Some didn't realize it stemmed from my profound religious belief in the afterlife, as they thought my psychic gift was just some kind of party piece that could be used to entertain them during their dinner breaks. They would often ask me, 'What has Angela got for us today, then?' It created a lot of frivolity, which I didn't mind at the time, as it seemed to lift their spirits, which was sometimes needed because of their stressful workloads. Others just didn't understand the context of it all. They didn't know I was spending my weekends and evenings serving Spiritualist churches up and down the length and breadth of the country. Those who I felt understood more were one or two of my black colleagues, and they would put it into some context by commenting about me 'prophesying'. There were times when colleagues' loved ones would come through from Spirit with a message during working hours, and I would, as usual, just have to pass it on regardless.

One came to a total non-believer, who always seemed disinterested in the subject. It was during a one-to-one supervision session with my manager. As we were about to finish the session, thoughts came interrupting my mind. I had a feeling a young man wished to communicate. I then had a glimpse of a vision. The outline of his spirit was standing beside my manager, as she asked whether there were any other issues to be discussed. I found myself replying, 'Yes, Jean. Alan, your first love, wants to be remembered.' I said it spontaneously.

'Oh, Angela!' she gasped, as it took her breath away. The message had obviously struck a chord. She looked shocked and was stuck for words – something I thought I would never see! She seemed flustered as she scooped up her files in her arms and very quickly fled the room. After that she never once brought up the subject and never looked at me again in the same light. I definitely gave her food for thought.

I felt that Bridget's influence this time was about educating the staff. Including management!

We are all actually born with a Spirit Guide or Guardian Angel. We are allocated them from birth. Their role is to watch over us and to guide us along our pathways. They are highly evolved souls who have earned the wisdom of many lives. They help us to explore our own capabilities. And help us to aspire to reach our full potential. They are with us throughout our life's journey.

Sometimes it's during tests of endurance that their influence can be known and their presence can be felt. They knowingly, and wisely, pick which moments to interact with us. They guide us to our destination. They play a part in our soul's development. Helping us through life's lessons. We may be experiencing something that they experienced in their own physical existence here on the Earth plane. Who better to guide us than someone who really knows? They are spiritual role models. For most people they work almost silently and invisibly. Influencing our thoughts, as this is the way they communicate.

We can get to know our Guides through meditation and prayer. Some people are aware of their Guide's existence from a very early age, as I was – blessed to know them. Our Spirit Guides can change according to what we are experiencing at a particular time in our lives. It may be a case that we need the strengths and qualities of a different Guide. It is then that our Spirit Guides will change.

There may be similarities between you and your spiritual being. It is not only the case that we genetically inherit characteristics from our own fathers and mothers. I find that we can liken ourselves to the characteristics of our Spirit Guides. There is an actual spiritual attachment. Their personality can influence our thoughts, our words and our actions.

Sometimes it is not unusual to have more than one Guide. It may be the case that we may need the strengths and qualities of two distinct Guides. It is not unusual for me to be aware of and mention the 'other' nun in my life. I regard this other nun as a highly evolved soul, who only came to visit me at poignant moments on my journey. The first time she spoke to me was in my dreamstate, when I was a child in the convent children's home. She has not spoken since as clearly, and certainly not during daytime hours.

As I was receiving healing from a Spiritualist healer, sitting relaxed as I felt the radiating heat from their hands, I felt myself drifting off into a meditative state. I saw in my mind's eye a picture of my familiar visitor, one of my nuns. There she was, this time not in her usual attire. She wore a white headdress. She spoke to me and said, 'My name is Thérèse and you'll find me in a book.' She spoke with a French accent.

The vision disappeared. Her visit was short and sweet. She had come and gone so quickly. I had recognized her face, though. I was left feeling very intrigued by her visit. Who exactly is this lady? What did she want? And what was this book? It left me with the impression that I needed to search and make enquiries about her to find out more. She certainly gave me food for thought.

I then became conscious of where I was as the healing session came to an end. The healer then said something strange, which confirmed Thérèse's visit to me.

'I must tell you I'm not mediumistic like you, but as I lay my hands on you I "received" a clear picture in my mind of a nun. The strange thing about her was she was not dressed in the usual habit, as she had a white headdress on.'

I squeezed her arm and said, 'Thank you for telling me that. I saw her, too. Isn't that amazing?' We both agreed, as we were both touched by her communication. This visit had a strong significance, and I just had to find out why Thérèse's spirit had come to both myself and the healer, as if to make doubly sure that I would make further enquiries. Spirit does not use that amount of energy unless there is a good reason or purpose.

Excited by what I was given, I took it on board for the days and weeks that followed to try and find more information about Theresa, or Thérèse, as she called herself. She clearly told me I would find her in a book. I spent what spare hours I had combing through books in my local library. After a few weeks my obsession was diverted by the usual daily family crises in my busy life. Or you could say I 'gave up the ghost' for a while! Pardon the pun.

Some 18 months later I was in a Catholic bookshop, one I would often visit to buy my usual supply of crucifixes. A crucifix is something I always leave behind me after a Soul Rescue, as it is one of the greatest symbols of protection. Soul Rescues is another aspect of my work, which is a specialist area in which I have witnessed some wondrous results over the years. It's a subject I have gained much experience in, and my discoveries have been so vast that there's no room to include them in this book!

As I walked up to the counter, the assistant couldn't help but notice the number of crucifixes I held in my hand. 'Spreading the word, are we?' she quipped.

'Oh yes, in a roundabout way,' I said.

I felt I'd be there all day if I started to explain myself. But then I happened to glance down and spotted a familiar face on the cover of a book. It was a picture of a pretty young woman with dark hair done up in a bun and she was wearing a dress with a high-necked, buttoned collar. I could recall her face but nothing else. I was a little confused as to who she was and asked the assistant, who must have thought I was changing the subject as I pointed to the book and said, 'Excuse me, please, can you see that book with the picture of the lady on the front? She didn't happen to be a nun by any chance, did she?'

'Oh! Oh yes!' she replied. She looked at me as if she were surprised that I didn't know. 'You're only looking at St Theresa!'

Thérèse of Lisieux

Thérèse, my spirit guide, as a novice, aged 16

I was taken aback. I grabbed the book and looked through it. I was so excited about the thought of finding concrete evidence of my Spirit Guide's existence, I just had to buy the book, just in case it held some kind of hidden message. I couldn't tell the shop assistant about my findings, although I was bursting to – I knew she wouldn't understand. The look she gave me when I bought the crucifixes was odd enough!

I left the shop feeling elated. That evening I sat up half the night trying to read most of it and found that there were quite a few synchronicities and coincidences in the book that were uncanny.

Theresa (as I call her), or Thérèse of Lisieux, was born in Normandy, France, in 1873. There was a lot of recorded photographic history of her in the book. One particular photograph was just as I had 'seen' her 18 months before, in her white headdress as a novice nun. 'Remarkable!' I thought. 'Why is she with me?' I asked myself, feeling rather humbled by it all.

It became more apparent as I read her book. In essence, she was a young nun who'd written a book, her autobiography, about her spiritual experiences and her own sense of 'spirituality'. The book was called *Histoire d'une Ame* ('The Story of a Soul'). That was the 'psychic' or 'soul' connection between the two of us. Her spirit was trying to encourage and guide me to write about my own very spiritual experiences, and I am sure without doubt that her spirit has influenced and helped me with the words of this book. God bless her. And Sister Bridget, too.

Murder and Crime

My eventual involvement in crime was an integral part of my development, though it seems being able to help on crimeinal cases such as murder is a fundamental part of the process of healing that the use of mediumship offers. Some of my experiences have involved very powerful visions – some of which have been accompanied by communication from the murdered victim's spirit. These powerful visions are very vivid and filled with colour. It is like watching a video recording of the events, a spate of flashing visions piecing together the facts of the crime. Facts that I would know very little or nothing about beforehand.

Perceiving these visions is like looking at pictures through a layer of Cellophane – and they may only last for a few seconds. These visions have been most powerful when my attention, through Spirit, has drawn me to a particular crime. The situation has been 'instrumented' so as to lead me to become involved in some way. When I'm actually at the scene of a crime I not only have a series of related visions but in some cases the murder victim has communicated to me, telling me who was involved in their murder.

Each case produced very different ways and strengths of communication, varying in intensity, as it is about energy levels and vibrations, just like any other time when mediumship is used. But I can say that I believe that those very vivid, clear visions come through no other source than the power of God alone. This doesn't mean to say that every case will be solved, but fortunately on the cases where I have been involved I have been able to give remarkable results.

Sometimes it is important for me to work 'blind', knowing little or nothing about the circumstances. Whatever I then receive through Spirit will be compared against the facts.

The way I help in the process is by initially confirming particular lines of enquiry and facts that have already been noted. Through Spirit, I receive specific information on how events happened, stating who was involved, and then information on what will eventually unfold and whether the case will be solved. Anyone with an ounce of sense knows that a psychic's evidence will not be admissable in court, but psychics are still used, if only to confirm lines of enquiry. We have been an essential tool in the process of gathering evidence. Most of all, I have been blessed to be able to give hope to families and the police. It would be a perfect world if every case could be solved, but those unsolved cases are a necessary part of the pain of someone's journey.

I have never approached any police force or victim with information regarding any crime. More often than not the initial contact comes from victims and victims' families. My information about the crime will then be fed back to the police. It is then up to the individual officer to take on board the information or make the decision to seek further help from me.

I know my information has startled police officers in the past. It has been like a 'blow' to their logical minds, as the majority of them have been totally sceptical. But one superior officer once told me that he was prepared to use any tool to help gather his evidence, and I was one of those tools. I admire him and other officers who can open their minds to accept help from beyond their own sources of logic and hard facts.

One of my first connections to crime came when a lady named Sue telephoned me, stressing that she had to talk to me urgently and that she had something she desperately needed to tell me. We arranged to meet up at her home in Birmingham. She explained that it had been a few years since our first meeting – when she had been with a group of friends who were having private sittings with me. She said she'd been a complete sceptic back then, as she proceeded to tell me about her sitting. She began:

'Angela, you may not remember, but you brought through a communication from my grandfather, whom you described to a "T". You went on to tell me that I would marry a man with links to the Yorkshire area. And you told me I would start my own cleaning company, which I did, and it is very successful, as you predicted! During the sitting you became alarmed and asked me if I knew a conman. I felt a little bit insulted and said that I did not know any such kind of person! And I told you that I would

certainly not associate myself with any such person, but you went on and gave me some kind of warning of a conman, and you stressed it was "a conman in the true sense of the word"! Those were your exact words – "conman in the true sense of the word". You then asked me if I knew somebody named Lionel, to which I answered no. You also asked if I knew a Gordon. These two names held no relevance at the time. You then said that you could definitely "see" a man behind bars!

'*At the time I was rather defensive as I insisted that I certainly didn't know any such person. This is the reason for us meeting again, and I must tell you, taking into consideration my initial scepticism, I am now a great believer in the Spirit World and in you, and it is only because of what you told me. I was completely amazed as everything you said to me has completely come true!*'

She spoke nineteen to the dozen – she couldn't get her words out quickly enough as she went on to say:

'*I met and married my man from Yorkshire. It was approximately six months into the marriage that my husband phoned me one day at work to ask me what time I would be coming home that evening. When I did return home, I found all his personal belongings had gone, the car had gone, and subsequently I found that our bank accounts had been emptied! It was then that I remembered the words of your sitting. I obviously reported it to the police. I was suffering from shock. But during that evening I remembered what you'd said about the conman. I searched the house for the tape recording that you made of the sitting I had had with you. It revealed so much. Everything you'd said had come true, and things that weren't significant at the time later turned out to make complete sense. It was five months later they found the scoundrel! They discovered he had conned other women in different parts of the country. I knew him as Steve, but to my complete and utter surprise his real full name was Lionel Gordon. The two names you gave me! And he is now serving five years in prison, hence the man you "saw" behind bars. You are absolutely amazing with your accuracy and detail! Next time I will listen to my grandfather!'* Sue was made aware of my sense of humour as I replied, 'Oh my God! My friends in the Spirit World must want me to be some kind of Miss Marple!'

Joking aside, looking back on this sitting it was one of the first times that my attention was drawn to criminal activity, and it appears it was an indicator of things to come.

I went home that evening eager to share my experiences with my elder children, as they would always find time to hear of my 'adventures', as they, too, are fascinated by the work I do. At times, though, they don't grasp it fully, and that is when they will make light of it, which they did in this case by calling me 'the Miss Marple of the Spirit World'. It was a title that stuck for a while.

It is often through chance meetings that something of great significance happens but its relevance may not come to pass until much later – in this case, years later.

Once I was browsing in a local clothes shop in town, assuming I was having a well-deserved day off from those people of the Spirit World. Unfortunately, if you are an instrument of the Spirit you never know when you are going to be used! As I was browsing I looked over to the other side of the shop and felt very drawn to speak to the female assistant behind the counter, who was standing alone. As I approached I could see by the label on her lapel that she happened to be the manager. Totally 'inspired', I found myself saying to her, 'Excuse me, love, I have a message for you.' She looked at me, puzzled. I went on to say, 'I know you will understand this. Don't worry, I am a local medium.'

I then asked, 'Who is Carole?'

'That's my name! Oh yes! Yes! Carry on, I'm a great believer in all this stuff,' she said, describing it rather baldly! She looked at me, apprehensively awaiting my response.

'I am being made aware you are trying to escape from a man who is suffering from manic depression, who can be violent at times. Be careful! You must play it safe! Safe is the word!' I said.

'Yes! I am planning to get my belongings out while he is at work!' she replied.

I then interrupted her and said, 'Don't worry, I can see you going to a house that has very tall trees outside.'

'You seem to be describing the Women's Refuge, which I am considering going to!' she said.

I reassured her by adding, 'Don't worry, everything will turn out for the best in the end, but I sense and "see" there is a tall man around you with a black moustache, who seems to be surrounded with a lot of black cars. He has been sent to help you.'

She smiled and confirmed, 'That's an old friend, he's an undertaker! I can't believe you've just said that to me!' She held my hand and thanked me for the reassurance.

As I was leaving the shop, I got to the door and turned back and said, 'I can't see you staying in retail work for long. I can see you managing a pub!'

She looked at me and said, 'No love, I can't see myself doing that. I did it years ago!'

'Anyway, my love, goodbye,' I said, 'and just remember that your mother is watching over you!'

I saw her expression change as she welled up with emotion. I came away feeling satisfied and humbled that once again I had completed a mission on behalf of God's work – and all in good time to do the weekend shopping!

It was approximately 18 months later, when I was looking for a suitable venue for my granddaughter's christening party, that I walked into a local public house to find Carole, the lady from the shop, standing behind the bar!

'Well, well!' I said. 'This does not surprise me!' She looked at me in great surprise. When she realized who I was, we both laughed!

'Fancy meeting you again. Isn't that strange you told me I would work in a pub again?' she said. She went on to explain that this was her new partner's idea, to go into brewery management. She kindly offered me the function room at a discount price in return for the help I had given her in the shop! Then she looked at me and said with a cheeky grin on her face, 'While you're here, you can't tell me where I am going to next, can you? as I'm only here temporarily.'

I then had a clear picture in my mind, as I replied, 'I can see a cream-painted public house with a stretch of water at one side and a field at the rear.'

'Really? I'll just have to wait and see what happens then, and I will let you know,' she said.

I left the pub feeling that I had established more than a casual acquaintance with Carole.

A few months later, she telephoned to tell me that she had now moved to the public house I had described, which had a canal at the side and fields at the back, but she added that it had been a couple of weeks after they'd moved in that workmen from the brewery came to render it and paint it all cream!

Carole soon became a regular client. I found her a jolly person with a good sense of humour, who was strong-spirited and uplifting. A personality, who would soon put a smile on your face. We tended to laugh at the same things.

She had not been settled long in her new premises when she telephoned me to say that she had had a robbery at her pub. She began to tell me, 'I had to call you because I know you will be able to help me. We've had a robbery. They took the only money on the property, which was in the gambling machines, which the robbers smashed up in the process.' In a half-joking manner she added, 'Why don't you come down and put your arms around the gambling machines and tell me what you sense and feel?'

We laughed at the thought of me hugging a gambling machine! Nevertheless, I agreed to help. I arrived at the pub just before opening time and stood in front of the gambling machine, which towered above me. I touched it and this triggered a vision in my mind's eye.

'Oh! Carole, I can see two men standing here. One tall, with a thick head of dark hair; the other short and stocky, with a bald head. They stood here,' I said, as I pointed to the spot, but then I automatically turned round and pointed to the other machine and continued to say, 'There was a third man, smashing up the other machine at the same time.'

'Oh my God, Angela, you are describing exactly what has been captured on the CCTV camera! There is no way you could possibly know that! You're just amazing!'

In a flash, I said to her, 'Yes, but, Carole, these men are going to have the cheek of the devil and return to this pub and buy a meal, as I feel they often frequent this pub anyway!'

I asked her to call me if anything happened. My visit was short and sweet. I left and went about my daily business. A few days later, I just happened to be working in that area and decided to visit Carole for a quick cup of tea and a chat. As I approached the bar, I saw three men sitting round a table eating a meal. I had to look twice at them before I began to realize who they were, and I 'sensed' the shape and size of them married up with what I had seen in my vision. I could see Carole was not in the bar. I asked the bar person to give her a call quickly, to say that I was there and could she come as I had something important to show her?

Carole seemed pleased to see me. I immediately pointed out the three men and asked her what she thought of them. She replied, 'They're the men on the

CCTV film! I have no doubt about that.' Carole went and phoned the police and the three men were arrested.

It was this same Carole who called me in desperation in May 2003 to tell me of a murder that had been committed at the Royal Oak pub in Pelsall. She told me, 'Oh, Angela, they have murdered the owner, Mick Hughes. He was such a lovely man and he did not deserve to die this way. I am sure you will be able to help. Why don't you pay them a visit?' she said, pleading with me to go.

'I can't just go down there and present myself on the doorstep. I will look such a fool!' Then I explained, 'I believe if I am meant to go, I will be told in some way through Spirit communication of some sort.' With that I made a promise. 'I will see what happens,' I said.

It was a couple of weeks later and I had almost forgotten about Carole's request. I was visiting the Arthur Findlay College in Stansted. While I was relaxing in the garden by the big oak tree, in an almost meditative state, I suddenly heard my late father's voice loud and clear in my ear! All he said was, 'What about this murder?' He was almost shouting. His voice seemed to echo in my head. It was almost a command. I knew I just had to go. It was so loud and clear. I surrendered by saying out loud, 'OK, I'll go!'

I planned that on my return I would have to pay the Royal Oak pub a visit. In fact, it turned out to be the following day! It was shortly before opening time that I drove up to the pub, parked in the car park, turned off the engine and sat quietly as I said a prayer and asked for guidance. I glanced over at the pub and there in my mind's eye I had my first of a series of visions connected with the murder! I could 'see' three men climbing up a black wrought-iron fire escape, clambering across a tiled roof, then over some railings onto a balcony. I watched them make their entrance through glass doors situated at the top of the building. If you can imagine, it was like watching a video recording in my mind.

With that first vision I felt confident enough to make my approach. I needed to tell someone what I had just seen! The pub door was locked. I knocked on the door. It was answered by a lady looking rather distraught. It became obvious to me that she was the victim's business partner.

'Can I help you?' she said. 'We are not open yet.' I introduced myself: 'My name is Angela McGhee. I am a medium, and I must tell you that I'm aware of your troubles and I may be able to help you.'

'A medium!' she said, startled. She explained that she had only been talking about mediums only the day before.

I went on to describe that first vision I had encountered in the car park. I could see by the look on her face that she was taken aback with what I had described. 'My God, of all the doors you could have mentioned, those glass ones, that is how they entered the building!'

She then asked me if I would like to come in and look around. As we approached the staircase, I had yet another vision, this time of chairs that had been toppled over. I told her about this.

'That's interesting, because the glass doors where they entered are those of the restaurant, and that's where there were chairs toppled over!' she answered.

As we entered the restaurant, where the chairs and tables had been moved during the process of police forensic investigations, I glanced at the near-empty room and could see three doors leading off. I pointed at one of the doors and 'sensed' I needed to go into that next room. 'Can I go through here?' I asked her. 'Of all the doors to pick, that is the door to the living quarters, but hold on, I must secure my dog!' she said. Little did I know at the time, but she confessed to me later that while she went through to the other room ahead of me she was actually putting rugs over the blood stains in the living quarters, to test my abilities. She doubted the power of my Spirit allies – which is understandable.

I entered a corridor with several rooms leading off, and felt very drawn to one bedroom in particular. As I stood in the doorway I had a vision of two men struggling with each other, splattered with blood. I looked up at her and said, 'This is where a struggle took place.'

I continued into the bedroom. I glanced over to the window and there, under the window, on the floor, I could 'see' the victim's blood-stained body!

'This is the place where Mick passed and this is where the body was found lying.' I looked across at the woman. Her face was ashen and she was shaking.

'How do you know? How do you know all this?' she said in disbelief. I reassured her again who I was and what sort of help we are able to obtain from the Spirit

World. I turned quickly, as my thoughts were interrupted by a 'flash' of vision. I could see three men running down the corridor, one of them carrying something about the size of a shoebox. This vision I described in detail to her. She confirmed by telling me that the safe that was stolen was the size of a shoebox. She was beginning to really listen to what I had to say! All of a sudden I felt a 'presence'. I could see Mick, the victim, standing in front of me. He was holding up a thick gold bracelet in his hand for me to notice! I turned to her and said, 'Mick is trying to tell me that there is something about a thick gold chain bracelet, connected with this robbery.' She paused for a while as she seemed to fathom out her thoughts.

'Oh!' she said. 'We had a robbery three weeks prior to this one, where his bracelet went missing!'

I could also 'hear' Mick in my mind, telling me something about her son, which he repeated. I sensed her son was connected with this incident. I became silent for quite a while, mulling over in my mind the appropriate words to choose, for obvious reasons. I said to her, 'There are three men involved in this incident, and Mick knows one of them very well! He has actually drunk with them and they are people who frequent this pub, who are in the "know" and, somewhere, there is woman connected with the robbery as well!'

'I can't see a woman involved with this!' she said, dismissing the idea.

'Well, my love, I can only give you what I receive,' I replied.

She then held on to my arm and said, 'Please, please tell me this is going to get solved!'

My reply to her was, 'Four months from now, three men and a woman will be rounded up.'

I began to make my exit. I felt that I had done what I had been sent to do. As I was leaving, we went downstairs through the bar. The woman seemed dazed but could not thank me enough. She asked me to wait while she turned to the barman and asked him for a pen and paper, so that she could write her number down for me. I glanced at the barman and a cold shudder went through my body. My Spirit Guides were telling me, 'This is her son!' He passed paper and pen to her. She wrote her telephone number on it and gave it to me and said, 'If you get anything else, please contact me.'

I left in a hurry. I remember saying to myself, 'My God, why have you shown me all this?' My thoughts were that this experience would stay with me. I wasn't prepared to go to the police. It was such a profound spiritual experience that I chose to use it as an example in my addresses from the rostrum at the Spiritualist churches that weekend. I do believe that it was someone from the church congregation who fed the information to the police. Hence the call that I had a week later. The voice of a Detective from Bloxwich Police Station, who said, 'Hello, Angela! There is nothing to worry about! My colleague and I would like to come and talk to you about the murder at the pub in Pelsall, which I believe you have made a visit to recently?'

'No problem, tomorrow morning would be fine,' I replied.

They arrived the next day on my doorstep and introduced themselves, flashing their ID cards like something out of *The Sweeney*! I had never had detectives call before. I invited them both in. As they sat down and before they could speak, I had to make one thing clear – I wanted to know why they had come to question me!

'Before you ask any questions, lads, I want to ask *you* a few questions first,' I said. They looked at me, puzzled. 'I want to know whether you have any beliefs? Do you believe in God or the afterlife? Do you have a belief in anything unseen, some faith at all?'

The older detective replied, 'I understand where you are coming from, Angela, as I have been to see Colin Fry, the TV medium – but the wife took me!' he added, almost blaming his wife for this 'irrational' behaviour!

I looked at the other, younger detective to hear what he had to say. 'Sorry, love, I just believe in what I see,' he said apologetically.

'You know I feel sorry for people like you, as there must be some kind of void in your life somewhere, but anyway, each to their own!' I said.

That morning they spent a few hours with me. I initially gave them a little lecture about the different aspects of mediumship and also the work that I do, in the hope that they would grasp some kind of understanding.

I went on to describe, step by step, what I had seen at the scene of the crime. I watched them as they looked at each other in surprise. I had them scratching their heads and smiling. You could see they were beginning to question their own beliefs for a moment or two! The time spent wasn't so much them asking me questions but them listening to what I had to say! The only questions they asked me were to clarify that I had not been to the public house before. They never relayed any information to confirm anything that I was saying, but the occasional grin indicated something to me! After a couple of hours I thought they might have had enough of me lecturing them alongside giving them details of what I had 'received' when I'd visited the scene of the crime.

'Right then, lads, what do you conclude?' I said, looking to the older one for a reply.

'You are telling us things that are on file, things that only those people who are involved would know!' he said.

I jokingly replied, 'Well, are you going to arrest me then, as I know too much?' They smiled. I suddenly had a second thought and said, 'Thank God you know I am a medium!'

The older detective replied, 'Besides that, Angela, where are your cards?'

'Cards? Cards? I don't read cards!' I said defensively. 'All my information comes from the Realms of Spirit!' I said, thinking that my efforts had not been understood.

'No, no, Angela! You misunderstood me! I mean your business cards! As I'm sure the wife will be in touch!' he said.

I then turned to the younger detective and said, 'What about you, the total non-believer? What do you conclude?' I was very interested to find out, as he had stated that he was a complete sceptic. He looked at me, smiled and reached out his hand to shake mine; as he did, all he said was, 'I find you fascinating!'

I like to believe that I was opening up a 'chink of light' in his thoughts. With that I handed them a business card and in return they wrote their numbers on a notepad, handed it to me and said, 'If you get anything else, just let us know.' I had certainly given them a lot to think about.

A few days later, when I awoke, I had a vision of a picture of a dolphin. I sensed this was connected with the crime. I was also given a three-lettered nickname that sounded like 'Daz' or 'Gaz', and was compelled to call the police and give them the information. I rang the detectives. The younger one answered and I gave him the additional information. The detective confirmed that there was a public house called the Dolphin in the Bloxwich area. I also added that I sensed that something significant would happen within a few days.

I was pleased to read a few days later in the local paper that the police had found the empty safe in the canal situated behind a pub called the Dolphin in Bloxwich. Although I was pleased, I took it all in my stride and carried on with my daily work.

Another connection was made a couple of weeks later when a lady named Carol rang from the other side of town. She said she had a group of friends who would like to have a sitting with me and could I visit her, at her home, as there was so many of them? She went on to say that she had chosen me, even though she had been given four other mediums' names and numbers, but it was my name she felt very drawn to.

It was during Carol's sitting that I began to feel the build-up of a 'presence'. I felt her mother was in Spirit. I could hear her mother talking. She mentioned the place where she used to live and some of Carol's childhood memories, which Carol was clearly moved by. I was hearing the name 'Mick' being called. Her mother in Spirit was trying to tell me that she had someone known as Mick with her. But her mother was also insisting that his name was Michael, not Mick, I told Carol.

'That's right,' she said, 'she would only ever call him Michael, although he was known to everyone else as Mick.'

I then had a clear vision: it was Mick Hughes, the victim from the Pelsall pub murder. I gasped with surprise and told Carol who I could see. I then said, 'You must be connected in some way, as there is so much love being sent to you.' Carol looked at me with her eyes full of tears and said, 'Yes, that is my brother and my mother you are talking about!'

I could hear Mick say loudly, 'Justice! Justice! Justice!'

I told Carol he would see true justice, in the form of the killers getting the maximum sentence, which I felt would be the outcome of the case. Mick also went on to say something about going to Stafford. I asked Carol what the Stafford connection was. She said that she didn't know.

I went on to say that I could see a picture of the family standing together waving their fists in the air in triumph. I told her not to worry as I felt that Mick would get justice.

The outcome was that, four months to the day of my initial visit to the pub, the police arrested and charged three men and a woman for Mick's murder. One of the men had been known to the late Mick Hughes, as it was his business partner's son.

The Stafford connection then became apparent, as the court case – which was initially booked at Birmingham Crown Court – was transferred two days before the hearing to Stafford Crown Court. Hence Mick saying he was going to Stafford. This is where justice took place. I have no doubt that Mick was watching and listening to every word. Each of the three men was found guilty of murder and sentenced to serve no fewer than 20 years. The woman was found guilty of a lesser offence.

My final vision with regards to this case was confirmed in a picture in the local newspaper when justice had been done. It was just as I'd 'seen' it: the family standing on the Court steps, their fists punching the air in triumph! It was at that moment that I felt my work was complete.

I felt humbled and moved by the sheer power of the whole experience. I was touched again when, some months later, while in dreamstate, Mick Hughes visited me with a beaming smile on his face and thanked me. I woke up with his words of thanks in my ear. He is someone I will never forget.

It wasn't until three and a half years later, though, that I began to realize that my involvement in this case had a greater purpose. God was about to unfold the greater picture! I had a telephone call from an assistant producer from ITV, representing the Canadian film company Cineflix. A young lady on the other end of the phone said that they were filming a documentary series about mediums who have helped solved crimes with police detectives.

'I hear you're a crime-solving medium. Have you any good stories to tell us?' she asked.

What instantly came to mind was the Mick Hughes story, which I began to tell her. She asked if I thought the family would speak to them and did I have a contact number for them. I told her that I did not think I had their number anymore, as it was so long ago. But my Guide was telling me to go and look in my own diaries, which I did. I found the number and then I passed it on to enable them to do some further research. She got back to me a few days later to say that they had spoken to Mick Hughes' sister and daughter and that they were willing to talk and take part in the documentary. I was touched by the thought.

I was told our obstacle would be the West Midlands Police, for they would need to release the facts of the case and the detectives involved might not be prepared to talk to the film-makers. It was a few weeks later when I was feeling that they hadn't been successful in obtaining the information they needed that the assistant producer telephoned me again, all excited, saying, 'Good news, Angela! The West Midlands Police have released the facts of the case and we have found one of the detectives involved, who initially visited you. He is willing to talk and he has been very complimentary about you.'

In fact when I asked which detective they had traced, they told me it was DC Mike Crump, the younger of the two. The one who'd seemed a complete sceptic! I was surprised that he was willing to talk publicly about my involvement.

The other total surprise was Detective Chief Inspector Ian Bamber, whom I had never met, who said he would be willing to be interviewed on screen.

'This looks like it's going ahead. There will be other meetings we will have to arrange with the producer and a date will be set for filming. I will be in touch!' my contact from the film company said.

I had to pinch myself ! I could not believe I was making a film, let alone one that was going to be shown worldwide! It really did hit home about my soul's purpose. My childhood prophesies were coming true.

The date was set for the start of filming. I understood that the detectives and family were being interviewed in a local five-star hotel. I assumed I would be asked to go next, but the director phoned me up and introduced himself. He explained why I wasn't being interviewed at the hotel. 'Ma'am,' he said with an American drawl, 'I wanted a venue somewhere special for you, somewhere more authentic. I've hired Dudley Castle for the day!
This will be the first of our venues.'

I chuckled at the thought!

I remember arriving and feeling the cold, as it was a chilly February afternoon. After introductions, I found the film crew very warm and friendly. I could relax and be myself ! I felt it wasn't long before we gelled as a team. We chatted away between shots, exchanging our beliefs and disbeliefs on the subject of psychic abilities.

They all soon became aware of my humour. While they were filming an interview with me, you could hear the sudden squeals of animals and birds of the castle zoo.

'What's that?' the director asked.

'It's the penguins,' I said. 'You know what they are saying, don't you?'

He looked at me with a wry smile, waiting for the punchline, as I said, 'Last one in is a chocolate biscuit!' He and the crew fell about laughing. You could see their hand-held equipment shaking. They appreciated my silly sense of humour!

It was only the warmth of my humour that was keeping me warm that day. I was almost suffering from hypothermia! The film crew were geared up as though they were on an Antarctic expedition and there was I in a very thin, smart trouser suit. I was so cold that it got to a point where I asked the filming to stop and said, 'Excuse me, Mr Director, can I ask you something? How come the detectives and the family got a five-star hotel in Sutton Coldfield and I get a draughty, windy castle, with no windows, in a temperature of minus 10 degrees?' trying not to sound too unappreciative!

'But, Ma'am, this castle cost more to hire,' he replied, as if to say 'Be quiet! You are costing us more money!'

'After all, Ma'am, you are the star!' he said, reassuring me, trying to pump up my ego as well as my temperature!

I loved every bit of filming and I was in awe of everything going on around me. There was a time when I was encircled by the director, the camera man and the sound man. For a split second reality dawned on me and I needed to express how I was feeling at the time. I turned and looked at all three of them in turn and said to the director, 'Ooh, I feel like Dorothy in *The Wizard of Oz*!'

The director laughed and said, 'Ma'am, I just love that analogy.' Each one of them laughed as they studied each other, looking for similarities to the famous characters of one of my all-time favourite films. We all agreed that the director had to be the lion, because of his curly mane of hair.

The day spent at Dudley Castle was memorable. They were such a great bunch of professional people. I never realized that filming took so long, but I enjoyed every minute.

One day's filming was spent with Mick Hughes' sister Carol, in her home. She made us very welcome. This was the first time I had met her since her sitting three years previously. She told me she still had the tape recording of the sitting and she filled me in on the things I had said, which I had totally forgotten about! She said that she could not get over how amazingly accurate I had been about the whole situation concerning her brother's murder.

While the crew were filming Carol's part, a lady photographer arrived and said that she needed to take photos for publicity purposes. After being introduced, we sat and chatted, while we waited for a convenient slot. She was intrigued about my 'gift', and asked me if I could 'sense' or 'receive' anything for her, as people quite often do when they first meet me. She had not quite finished her sentence when I could 'see' in my mind's eye the outline of an old lady sitting doing cross-stitch. I then said to her, 'I have an old lady here. I sense she is your grandmother. She is telling me that cross-stitch was her hobby.' I could see the surprise on the photographer's face.

'Yes! Yes!' she said. 'My grandmother did wonderful things with cross-stitch!'

'I believe that somebody here is getting married. She is talking of a wedding coming up,' I said.

The photographer beamed and said, 'I am getting married in two weeks.'

'On a beach in Scotland!' I said, alarmed, thinking about the cold weather.

'Yes,' she said with a delightful little titter.

I explained I could hear her grandmother shouting so loudly because she too was surprised that someone would be getting married on a beach in Scotland in the middle of February!

The photographer laughed.

'I am being given a name that sounds like Ferguson – No, sorry, I am being told it is Farquarson,' I said.

'My goodness! That is my father's name! His name is Farquarson,' she said. 'You are amazing!'

'Don't worry, regardless of the cold weather your grandmother will be at this wedding, too,' I said.

'Bless her and thank you. I can't wait to tell the family,' she replied. She grabbed my hand and thanked me over and over again – very quickly, as our cue was being called!

The documentary regarding my involvement in the case of Mick Hughes' murder was part of a TV detective thriller documentary series about real-life crimes that have been solved through the unlikely combination of hi-tech detective work and the paranormal power of a psychic. One of the greatest accolades I have ever received was given by Detective Chief Inspector Ian Bamber, whom I never met, giving a summary about me at the end of the programme. It was his initial decision to send two of his detectives to visit me and to ask me, as a medium, what I knew about the murder.

What he said warmed the cockles of my heart: 'If I wasn't a policeman and I found myself in the position of the victim's family, I would certainly have gone down the road to the "olive branch" of hope that Angela was able to offer.' He obviously understood something about mediumship, as it is all about hope!

Baz's Story

It was during a day's filming that I received a telephone call from a very distraught woman. 'Hello,' she said, 'is that Angela McGhee? I have been looking for you everywhere! My name is Sheila McKenna. I saw an article about you in *True Crime* magazine. I wonder if you could help me, please? We think that our son has been murdered. I would like you to come to Newcastle. I need to know more about his last moments. Please, please, can you help us?' she pleaded. 'Can you come tomorrow?' The woman was clearly desperate. I could sense her pain. I interrupted her and asked her to stop there. I explained that I was filming and was committed for the next few days. I also asked her not to tell me anything about her son or the circumstances surrounding his death. I explained I like to work 'blind'. I did not want

'Baz', Barry McKenna

The McKennas' home

to be told any facts to interrupt communication from Spirit.

Sheila arranged for me to fly up to Newcastle on a dayreturn flight, on the following Tuesday. It was the evening before, at bedtime, that I began to say my prayers, asking for guidance and help for Sheila McKenna and David, her husband. I begged God to guide me and asked to be his greatest instrument, so that I could help relieve some of their turmoil. That night my sleep was restless. My dreams were interrupted by a vision of an illuminated right arm. I awoke knowing that this was connected with their son's passing.

During the flight, I looked out of the aeroplane window and there above the clouds I saw the vision from my dream of the night before. I could see his right arm time and time again.

I was met at the airport by David McKenna. He looked a tall, strong man, but you could see the grief on his face as he welcomed me. He shook my hand and said that we would not be travelling too far to his home. As we got into the car, I said, 'David, there is something I must tell you. Since last night I have had a vision of an illuminated right arm. There is something about your son's right arm.'

He looked startled and gasped, 'Angela, I must tell you that the whole of this case involves an issue surrounding his right arm. My God! That is uncanny that you said that!'

As we were driving along, I felt a strong presence beside me. It was his son, and in my ear I heard a voice saying, 'It's Baz. It's Baz.' This was David's son's voice from Spirit.

'David, I can hear the name Baz. It's Baz. It's Baz.' I said.

I had fathomed the name clearly!

'Whey-aye!' he replied in his Geordie accent. 'That's my boy. He was known to everyone as Baz. You will see the flowers when we get to the house,' as he explained there were still floral tributes lying in the garden.

Baz's spirit was full-on communicating in my ear! I could hear him speak again as I turned to David and said, 'You have been married twice and got five children, so Baz tells me.'

David smirked and said, 'Yes, that's right.'

I heard Baz say in a loud voice that he lived by the church.

'By the church!. You live by the church, don't you David?' I said, as I continued to relay Baz's words.

'Yes, you could say that,' David said with a wry smile.

As I was driven along, I could see a church in the distance. As we approached, to my surprise, we turned into the churchyard. I then understood why David had laughed! His home was a beautiful grand old monastery, which was joined to the back of the church. It was called Hebburn Hall. A home which

David told me he had renovated himself. It was magnificent and I was taken into the large country kitchen, where I was met by Sheila, Baz's mum.

As she welcomed me, she gave me a big hug and held on to me for a while, as if her life depended on it. I could feel the warmth of her personality, but I could also sense her tears and heartache. I tried to keep my emotions intact, as I had work to do. David told Sheila what I had already told him about Baz. She could not get over the fact that I had given his nickname. I interrupted them and asked them to get me a pen and paper, as I felt Baz was urging me to continue. Sheila gave me a pen and paper and David went to fetch a tape recorder. As I sat on a chair in the kitchen, I began to write Baz's words. I could hear him as he was telling me it was an alcohol and heroin overdose that had caused him to pass over.

David and Sheila listened attentively. I looked at them both and told them what I'd received. They nodded in agreement. I was then told by Baz that he didn't want to go. He did not want to go! he shouted and repeated again. I knew then that there was something dreadfully wrong. I turned and said to David and Sheila, 'This is definitely an alcohol and heroin overdose. The hard fact is that Baz did not want to go. Someone else had a hand in Baz's passing. You will find that the outcome of the coroner's report will confirm this, as it will be left open as a suspicious death.'

'That is exactly what our thoughts are, but we need to know more about his last hours,' Sheila said.

I then had a vision – I was being shown a row of 10 houses overlooking a green embankment. I described what I saw to them both.

'Baz wants me to go where this place is. I feel this is one of the places he visited during his last few hours. In fact I feel it was a starting point to the last few hours of his life,' I said.

'You are describing his ex-girlfriend's house,' said Sheila. 'We believe he left there a few hours before he died that evening. I will get David to get the car and we will go there now,' she added.

As we drove through the estates of Newcastle we arrived at the row of 10 houses. It was just as I had 'seen'. As we pulled up outside the houses, I could hear Baz shouting the name 'Campbell, Campbell, Campbell' angrily. I could hear him loud and clear in my mind. I told Sheila what I was hearing. She looked alarmed as she replied, 'You tell my Baz from me, we know about
Campbell.'

'What is this about?' I asked.

'Campbell is one of his so-called friends, who moved in with Baz's girlfriend just weeks after his passing,' Sheila informed me.

Within a split second I could see the name of a road, Solway Road, written in my mind's eye.

'Take me to Solway Road,' I said to David, 'wherever that is, as I feel this is where Baz travelled.'

'My goodness,' he said, 'Solway Road is around the corner.'

As we drove there I then asked David to stop the car as I had another vision. I could see Baz getting out of a car in front of me. It looked as if he was arguing with someone who was in the car. I could see him walk off on his own, up the road. It was like watching a video recording but in broad daylight. I told David what I could see. He confirmed to me that one of Baz's friends had witnessed that incident, and that he understood it was a fact. The visions and communications began to flow. I urged David to continue to drive up the road, as I could see in my mind's eye a row of shops with flats above. One of them stood out. I noticed a window to one of the flats that seemed smoky. I continued to describe what I was 'receiving'.

As we parked up alongside the shops, the 'smoky' window became more apparent, as someone had made a feeble attempt to put an adhesive roll of Polaroid paper across the window which had bubbled up, hence the smoky look. This prevented others from seeing inside. As I continued to glance at the window, Baz's spirit was showing me inside the flat. I could see a sparsely furnished room with only a blue-patterned settee and one armchair. I could see Baz's body lying on the settee, as this is where he had died. I described what I could see to David and Sheila. They said that they had never visited the flat before and did not know what was in there.

David said he could get the keys so that we could have a look inside. He telephoned someone and had harsh words with them, demanding that he should bring the keys to him straight away. He then explained to me that the young man who was about to bring the keys of the flat was the young man who had stated that he was with Baz when he'd died.

David asked me not to mention who I was, as he said, 'If he asks, I will tell him you are a distant relative, but I would like you listen to what he has to say about those final moments and then to tell me what you can sense about him, if anything.'

The young man arrived, looking pale, dishevelled and gaunt. We sat together in the car and I had great difficulty in deciphering what he was saying because of his thick Geordie accent! I sat with him and sensed his fear and that he was covering up something.

After he had gone, I told David of the intensity of my feelings and the fact that he was hiding information. David said he was only aware of how frightened the young man was of him!

All three of us approached the entrance door to the flats. As we climbed the stairs, I had a vision of Baz staggering up the staircase. A thought came in – I sensed this vision of Baz was the second and final time he had visited the flat that fateful evening.

As we entered the flat, there was the blue-patterned settee and one chair in the sparsely furnished room, just as I had seen it. As I glanced at the settee, I could see the position of Baz's body, with the young man whom I'd just met sitting alongside him. This I described to his parents. But then, when I turned and looked at the single armchair, I could see yet another young man. I glanced and the vision continued to show itself. I could see this other young man running out of the room in a panic!

'David,' I said, 'there is another young man here,' as I pointed to the chair. 'There was another young man with your son when he passed. In fact, there were two of them with him!' I said.

'Are you sure?' David asked.

'Yes! Yes! I can only give you what I receive,' I said.

'What does he look like?'

'He is not too tall. Mousey-coloured hair, slim in the body and he is wearing a beige-and-brown chequered baseball cap, a blue bomber jacket and jeans. He looks younger than the young man whom we have just left. I feel this is who he's covering up for,' I said.

David replied, 'I think I know who he is! Your description is uncanny. It could be his younger brother that was with him, as they are quite often seen together.'

I then had another vision of Baz lying in a stupor holding up his right arm, as someone else injected him with a lethal dose of heroin. Hence the issue over his right arm.

I began to feel mentally drained. Also, Baz's spirit had stopped communicating and I felt my Spirit Guides were beginning to leave me. I began to sense David and Sheila's agony and felt it was time to leave.

David had taped everything I had said. He then paused for a long while as he sat on the settee in the exact place where Baz had taken his final breath. He stroked the arm of the settee, deep in thought. I sensed he was longing to sense and feel for himself Baz's spirit. I watched helplessly, thinking and wishing if only I could give him, for just one minute, what I could sense of his son's spirit. My emotions began to kick in and I felt a tear trickle down my cheek as I said, 'That is all I have for now, shall we go?'

David and Sheila began to pick themselves up emotionally as we stepped out of the doorway of the flat. Sheila glanced over and pointed to the flat opposite and said, 'How uncanny is that? My Baz was born there in that flat and he has now passed away in nearly the exact same place.' I thought to myself that Baz's life's journey was almost a full cycle of events. Which doesn't surprise me, as I have heard of so many similar synchronicities and stories!

They took me to lunch, after which we returned to Hebburn Hall, their grand house. As I sat in the lounge with David I could again feel Baz's presence. This time the purpose of his communication was to lift his parents in some way and to divert them away from the trauma of that morning's events. He wanted to help ease them by sending his love alongside memories of his childhood. I could sense Baz's true personality. I told them he was a bubbly, humorous character and was a very popular lad who had many friends here. He wanted me to relay to them that he was now with his grandma, his father's mother, whom he had met up with in the Spirit World. He began to produce memories of his childhood in photographic images in my mind. The first was of him as a young teenager, standing in front of a stone wall in the countryside. I began to describe this to David and said, 'I can see Baz in a photograph. He is telling me he is 12 years old. There is a large stone wall behind him. I hear Northumberland. Is Northumberland where the photograph was taken?'

'Whey-aye,' said David. 'I did take him to Northumberland when he was about that age. I can put my hand on the photograph, I know where it is. I will go and fetch it.'

On his return to the living room, Baz had already 'shown' me another photograph – one of his favourite memories. This time it was more recent. It was a photograph of him and several of his mates on holiday in Ibiza. I told David what I was receiving. He grinned and said, 'I think we have that one, too. I will go and look for it.'

He was so eager to go and find this other photograph! He returned smiling, holding it up in his hand as if he had found gold. He handed it to me. As I held it, I could hear Baz calling out his mates' nicknames: 'Bonna, Campbell, Sully.' I pointed to them in the photograph. David smiled, acknowledging all of Baz's friends' names.

Baz spoke of his funeral, saying he was overwhelmed by the amount of people who had turned up. I heard him jokingly almost shout, 'Bonna in a suit!' He was referring to his best friend, as if he could not get over the sight of him wearing a suit! I told David.

'That's right, Angela,' David said. 'It was the first suit he had ever bought, let alone worn! Baz would be amused at that sight! It was a sight for sore eyes!' he joked.

Then David seemed lost in thought. I emphasized to him that communication of this intensity comes only from a high vibration of love. It was Baz's love he wanted to convey, not only to David and Sheila, but to all his family and friends. As David sat there, I heard Baz say, 'Tell my dad I love him!' I felt this was something he would not have been able to say when he was here, as he would have put on a 'macho man' bravado act. David's expression changed, as his eyes filled up with tears. He then glanced at his watch, as he realized the time and reminded me that we should be making tracks to the airport.

It was during our journey back to the airport when David tried to express how he felt about the day's events. He seemed to be talking in riddles, as he asked me what car I would prefer to be chauffeured about in, given the choice. Confused, I said, 'What are all these questions in aid of?'

'Answer me!' he said. 'What would you prefer? A Jaguar, Bentley, Rolls Royce?'

I answered quickly, not knowing my answer was being influenced by my new friend Baz.

'Oh! I'd have a Roller,' I said.

'What colour?' he said.

I knew then that Baz was influencing my thoughts as I replied, 'Your Baz has just said, "Go for gold. It has to be a gold Rolls Royce."'

'Isn't that strange?' said David. 'I was offered a gold Rolls Royce when Baz was here. I wonder if it is still for sale!'

'What's this all about then?' I said.

'You're coming back to Newcastle,' he said, almost ordering me, 'and when you do, I will chauffeur you about in a gold Rolls Royce! That's a promise! That is how much your visit here today has meant to me! That is the least I can do. Besides that I am sure there are plenty of people here in Newcastle who would want to meet you.'

We said our goodbyes. The day had been full of events both remarkable and phenomenal. I shall never forget Baz.

I tried not to think of the sadness of it all but the sheer beauty of his communication instead. It overwhelmed me. There I was flying back home to relative normality. I could imagine my children no longer calling me the 'Psychic Detective' but the 'Flying Psychic Detective'. That would be my next title!

On my arrival home I got back into the routine of cooking dinner for my family when my footballing son arrived home and said, 'Where have you been all day, Mum? I have been trying to phone you.'

I gave him a look because I'd told him where I'd be that day. But as usual it must have been a case of 'in one ear and out the other'. So I said casually, 'Oh! I have just flown up to Newcastle-upon-Tyne, solved a murder and I am now back in time to cook your spaghetti Bolognese.'

'Yeah, yeah! Can you put cheese on the top, Mum?' The whole issue went over the top of his head. 'Back down to earth as usual,' I thought to myself!

Later on he asked me if I'd seen the 'Angel of the North' monument. 'No, unfortunately not,' I said.

'Never mind, Mum, you may not have seen the "Angel of the North" but they've certainly seen the "Angel of the South",' he said, trying to flatter me.

'What are you after, son?' I replied, knowing that his flattery usually had an ulterior motive! I held my breath, waiting for his reply: 'Can you lend us 20 quid, Mum?' 'How predictable he is', I thought!

It is moments like this that help to revive me and enable me to continue my work for Spirit. Humour is a quality and a coping mechanism that has helped me through my work, not only as a medium but in a number of stressful jobs I have had over the past 25 years in the caring profession. My job as a medium I see as just another caring role. It gives me great satisfaction as I have a greater insight into people's heartaches and troubles and I am able to gain wondrous results and sometimes the greatest satisfaction as I witness God's miracles at work.

I got a lovely surprise when Sheila and David invited me back to Newcastle for the weekend a few weeks later. I met many people and, of course, I was chauffeured about in a gold Rolls Royce, bought in memory of Baz's communications.

The *Psychic News*, the Spiritualists' National Union newspaper, was interested in Baz's story. Sheila McKenna gave permission for it to be published. The uncanny thing was we did not know exactly which week the story would be in the news, but, as with most things in life, I believe there is perfect timing. The story was not only front-page news on the week of Baz's birthday, but it just so happened that the Spiritualists' National Union's annual general meeting was held in the North East that week. It was as if Baz wanted to tell the whole of the North East he had spoken!

His spirit will always hold a special place in my heart. I didn't realize then, but as the months went past Baz would pay me short visits and sometimes would help with communication from other souls like himself. Young men of the Spirit World.

The next unexpected visit happened as I was delivering a service at the David Jones Centre, a Spiritualist church in Stafford. I saw Baz's smiling face flash up in my mind's eye. It was when I was scanning the congregation in order to give my next communication. I instantly knew I was 'seeing' him for a purpose! As I looked at a woman I could hear Baz say in my Spirit ear, 'She, too, has a son in the Spirit World and here he is!' It is almost as though he 'opens the door' for them. I went on to give a message to the woman from her 22-year-old departed son.

That is when I began to realize that Baz now had a role to play in the Realms of Spirit, in helping other young men to communicate to their loved ones here. His role also reflects his personality, as he was such a popular person. I understand that when we pass to the Realms of Spirit, our personality stays the same. There is no doubt that Baz has now made many friends in Spirit World, as he did in this life.

It was several months later that I had a call from Sheila McKenna. She telephoned me to tell me that it had been confirmed that the young man I had met in the car that day had confessed that his younger brother was in the room with him on the night when Baz had died.

I would like to thank Baz for his love and help. May his good work continue. Bless him, his parents and family.

Murder via Text

It is not always necessary to visit the scene of a crime to feel the energies and receive Spirit communication about solving the crime, as I learned from the following incident.

I was at home when I received a text message from a young woman called Yvette. In the text she stated that her mother had been murdered in July 2005, and that no one had yet been found responsible. She pleaded for my help.

I thought to myself, 'I may be spiritually minded, but I am not technical!' – so I decided to call her back, as texting is not my thing! I asked her not to give me details of her mother's murder and also asked if it would be possible for me to visit the scene of the crime. She said that it would only be possible to stand outside *near* the property where the murder had taken place, as her mother was murdered at her workplace and the building was now boarded up. We arranged that I would travel to Shropshire to meet her a week later.

One evening the week before my visit I was sitting engrossed in a TV programme when my enjoyment was interrupted by a vision of a young man wearing a baseball cap, standing in front of a modern terraced house which stood close to the road. I sensed that he was about 22 years old, and I heard repeatedly, and also sensed, there was something very disturbing about this young man and that this murder had been premeditated. It was not a murder by chance. I became nervous about what I would see during my visit, as I thought I was already connecting very strongly. But there was timely significance as to why I was already receiving.

This vision interrupted my daily chores for the several days that followed, convincing me that it was connected with Yvette's mother's murder. The day before I was due to travel I received a phone call from Yvette.

'Hello, Angela? I have something to tell you,' she said eagerly. 'There is no need for you to visit tomorrow, as they have found someone responsible for the murder and the police have now charged them.'

'That's wonderful news, Yvette, but please stop there. I need something confirming. Since we last spoke I have been receiving a recurring vision and thoughts. The vision is of a young man wearing a baseball cap, standing in front of a modern terraced house close to a road. I believe him to be 22 years old. I have also sensed that there is something very disturbing about him. And it was, I understand, a premeditated murder?'

'I can't believe what you have just said!' said Yvette. 'You have taken my breath away! I must tell you that I have always thought that my mother was murdered by an older man for some reason. Apparently the man they have charged *is* 22 years old, and he *does* wear a baseball cap! Another astonishing thing about what you are saying, Angela, is that you are actually describing the house where he lives! There is a picture of it in today's local newspaper, and what you are saying about him being disturbed – my God! He seems very disturbed, as I believe that when the police raided his property they found computer files that he quite often frequented one of these sickening sites that tell people how to murder someone.'

'It must be awful for you, Yvette, to have had your mum taken like that, but at least you can gain some comfort that they have caught and charged him and that I can give you the confirmation that they have the right person,' I said.

'Thank you for that. Thank you so much. But besides all this, I would really like to meet you, Angela, as I am a Spiritualist at heart. You are amazing!'

'We may get to meet after all,' I said, 'as I am due to serve Oswestry Spiritualist church in a few months' time. I look forward to meeting you there.'

As I was just about to say goodbye, I was interrupted by 'thoughts' from Spirit and I said, 'Yvette, just quickly I want to say to you that your mum loved the song that you played for her at her funeral. I sense it was a song by Elvis?'

There was a long silence on the phone and then, in a quivering voice as she began to cry, Yvette said, 'We did play Elvis' song for her. Thank you for that, Angela, it means so much to me. I look forward to seeing you.'

The power and energy of Spirit communication never cease to amaze me. There has always been an element of surprise, not knowing when I will actually be used as an instrument. I honestly believe that the help I have given in murder cases has been of divine intervention. I can quite humbly say that I have been blessed. It overwhelms me and humbles me and I feel like a small droplet of water in God's great ocean, as I succumb to the power of his greatness.

A Double Case of Missing Persons

It was 12th July, 2001, near the end of my granddaughter's third birthday party, which was held at my home, when the phone rang and the strained-sounding voice on the other end said, 'Hello, Angela. Please, please, can you help me? My name is Michelle. I have met you before, as I have had a sitting with you. I am in a terrible situation and I just hope you can help me. My son Reece, who is six years old, has gone missing. He was playing outside my house and he has disappeared. I have reported it to the police and they have now been searching for him for the last couple of hours, but they haven't found him. I am petrified because it will soon be dark. Please, please help me! I just need you to tell me where he is if you can?'

At the time of the call, although we were throwing a party for my little granddaughter, we as a family were going through a very personal crisis ourselves. My son, who was 22 years old at the time and who suffers with a mental disability, had also been reported missing a couple of days earlier. He had gone missing before but had always returned hours later. We would often joke that he liked to go 'walkabout', but this time it was different.

I was beside myself with anxiety, for he had been missing for almost three days. During that time I'd prayed and begged and pleaded with God and my Spirit Guides to tell me of his whereabouts, but I'd received nothing. I believed at the time it was because I had gone into an emotional state of shock and was functioning purely on auto-pilot. I realized that family life had to go on while a nationwide search was in progress, and I tried to keep my mind occupied with the needs of other people around me, as this helped me cope and stopped my mind running riot with different scenarios relating to the possible whereabouts of my son. I could not stop the feeling of total helplessness. You couldn't explain to a three-year-old what was happening, so the party had gone ahead.

That evening I was booked to go onstage at a Wolverhampton hall to do a charity event. I couldn't let people down; besides, all I needed was my mobile phone to be at my side so that I could receive news at any time.

So my reply to the young mother, Michelle – after a long silence – was, 'My love, I am stressed out at the moment. I can't give you an instant reply, but I promise you that if I do "receive" anything I will call you straight away. I promise.' I wanted to end the phone call quickly, as I was surprised by the coincidence involving our sons.

There was I thinking my 'channel' was completely shut down while clearing up after the party, when I suddenly heard the voice of my Spirit Guide saying loudly, 'He is in a block of flats.' I instantly knew my Guide was referring to the young missing boy and I automatically reached for the phone to tell Michelle the news.

'Michelle, Michelle, it's Angela here. Is there a block of flats close by to where you live?' I asked. 'As I feel your son is in a block of flats.'

'Yes, yes! There is one just up the top of the road. I will have to go and tell the police to go and have a look. Thanks, Angela. I will call you back later and let you know if there's any news.'

Shortly after, she phoned with the good news that her son had been found in the block of flats, as I had said. Apparently he had been having a whale of a time, playing up and down on the lifts, oblivious to the fact that the whole world was looking for him!

It was then that I went to pieces. I started to shout at God and my Spirit Guides, 'You can tell me where someone else's son is, but where is mine? Where is mine? Where is he?' I demanded to know. I sobbed uncontrollably. There was nothing but silence that followed. There was no reply. I felt deserted. That usual feeling of hope, only just a flicker now, told me that there must be a reason why they were not speaking to me. I pulled myself together and prepared myself for that evening's charity event.

On stage I worked in the usual way, relaying messages from loved ones. During the interval an old woman approached me and said I had a wonderful gift. Reminding me how blessed I was, she told me that she, too, was a medium. She said that while I was working on stage, she could see a spirit of a lady dancing round me. She said she felt it was my grandmother.

'Thank you for that,' I said. 'That would be my grandmother Kathleen Murphy, on a stage, given half the chance, as she was a dancer in the old-time music halls in the 1920s.'

The woman then grabbed my arm and pointed her finger at my face, as if she wanted to tell me something more serious. 'Aah,' she whispered to me, 'you've been shouting at Spirit, so I am told. I must tell you, you will get your answer – tonight.'

I stared at her, totally speechless, as she disappeared into the crowd as quickly as she had appeared. She had obviously been sent to me.

After the show ended I drove home, thinking about what the woman had said. Maybe my Guides were using her as the 'channel' to get their message to me. I was praying that she would be right. As I turned the car into the road where I live, there was my eldest daughter looking anxiously up and down the road as if she was awaiting my arrival. I had barely got out of the car when she ran over to me to tell me the news that my son had been found safe and sound. What relief I felt as I burst into tears.

'Where was he? Where had he been? I need to know,' I shouted to my daughter as my relief turned to frustration. I felt there was a reason why I wasn't meant to know his whereabouts.

'It seems he went to London on an adventure, by the sounds of it, Mum,' she said.

I then knew the reason why I wasn't told by my Spirit Guides where he had gone, as they were protecting me from added anxiety because they knew how I felt, through personal experience, about how easily people can go missing in London and remain missing for many years. Suddenly the silence from Spirit made perfect sense to me.

Missing (in Spirit)

One cold January morning I had arranged to go to Bristol to meet the parents of a young man named Stuart, who had gone missing. That's all I knew about him – his name and the fact that he'd gone missing. This meeting had previously been delayed because of bad weather.

In the days in between it being cancelled and rescheduled, *Pick Me Up* magazine had telephoned me to say that they were interested in doing an article about me and my 'psychic detective' work. I told them I was about to embark on a missing person's case in Bristol, so they asked if they could meet up with the parents and myself, with the parents' permission, to witness me 'working' on a particular case.

The parents agreed and we all arranged to meet up at a hotel in Bristol. It was while I was turning off the M4 and approaching the hotel that I could see in my mind's eye a picture of a tall, thin young man with dark hair. I knew instantly this was the missing person and that the communication was coming from the Spirit World.

My heart sank as I already knew the answer to their plight. Their son was no longer a missing person, as it was clear he had passed to Spirit. I could hear him calling the name 'John'. I knew this was somebody close to him. I held this communication in my mind as we all met in the lounge of the hotel. Stuart's mother introduced herself by saying, 'Hello, Angela, I am Julie and this is John, Stuart's father.'

As we sat down, she handed me a small passport photograph of her son. It was the young man I had 'seen' as I'd turned off the motorway. I held the photograph and the communication began to flow as the parents listened and Sam, the reporter from *Pick Me Up* magazine, made notes.

Although there was a conflict going on in my mind, as I already knew this young man had definitely passed to Spirit, I was not prepared to tell his parents just yet. I needed to grasp, first, what their response would be.

'Julie,' I said, 'I feel your son was a sunny, warm character. He would be about 30 years old. He would have had some connection with the Army. I believe he spent six years in the Army? I sense there is something about the dates 20th and 21st April.'

'Yes, yes! Angela, I must tell you, he did spend six years in the Army and he will be 30 this year as his birthday is on 20th April, but 21st April is the day that we reported him missing. Go on! Go on!' she said as she was so eager to hear more.

'I can see a jetty going out into the water,' I said, as I could hear him in my ear, telling me he was in the water. I still wasn't ready to tell them as yet. Their son's spirit was taking me on a journey in my mind's eye to the place where he had lived. I went on to say, 'I can see a road going up a hill and a three-storey apartment block. I feel that he did not live here in Bristol, he lived near some kind of resort.'

'You are describing where he lives. He lives in an apartment overlooking the sea. It's not around here, as he actually lives in Plymouth.'

Stuart's spirit kept showing me the jetty in the water. 'Tell her, tell her,' I heard him say. 'You must tell her, I was in the water. You must tell I have passed. She needs to know,' Stuart's spirit insisted.

I sat in silence as his words and my thoughts went over and over in my mind. It was the hardest thing I would ever have to tell someone. How could I tell this mother that her son was dead? I chose the words the best way I could by saying, 'Julie, can I ask you something?' 'Yes,' she said eagerly.

'Can I ask you if you have ever thought or felt that your son may be in the Spirit World?'

She stretched out her arm and touched mine, as her eyes filled with tears, and said, 'Angela, I am 99 per cent sure that he is. I just need some confirmation from you.'

'I must tell you it is your son Stuart's spirit that is communicating all this information. He had already introduced himself to me in the car, just before I arrived. He is still here with us. He wishes to continue to communicate,' I added.

His parents looked at one another and held each other's hands tight. They both cried and my eyes welled up. I had to contain myself to enable me to 'receive'. I noticed the reporter begin to bite her lip. She, too, had been moved.

'Please, please go on,' Julie almost begged me to continue.

'Your son is telling me he suffered from bouts of depression. I sense a turmoil of mixed emotions within him. I feel he could have suffered from Post-traumatic Stress Syndrome as he had served in some kind of conflict,' I said. 'The water is very significant to his passing. I am being shown a jetty going out to sea. I can hear him say he is in the water! He is repeating this, but what is this about him being in the water before?' – I could hear him saying, 'I've been in there before.' I looked at his parents for some explanation.

Julie looked alarmed as she said, 'You wouldn't know this, Angela, but the police had dragged him out of the water six weeks before he went missing, as he must have made a previous attempt on his life then.' Sam, the reporter, dropped her pencil with the shock of what she had just heard. Stuart's spirit was urging me to communicate as I said, 'I am seeing an Army cap badge being placed on someone else's grave.'

'Apparently Stuart had placed his cap badge on his grandfather's grave sometime before,' Julie replied.

'I can reassure you that he is now with his grandfather, William,' I said. 'Before he goes, he wants to say he was at your wedding.' I questioned what I'd heard: 'Does that make sense?'

I looked at them quizzically, as this made little sense to me as I'd assumed they'd been married for many years already. They looked at me and smiled as Julie explained, 'I have recently married John, Stuart's father, for the second time! We met up again 20 years after our divorce, and we actually got married after Stuart had gone missing. It is nice to know he was there. I want to thank you, Angela, for all that you have done and said today. I can now go away and start to grieve properly.'

Just as I thought Stuart's spirit had stopped communicating, another thought came in just before he left.

'Stuart wants to give you a trail of red flowers,' I said.

She beamed a radiant smile, as she replied, 'I have just planted a red trailing bush in Stuart's name.' She thanked me again and they both hugged me as they left.

Although the information I received that day saddened all those involved, I gained some consolation from being able to give some closure to the case. And this was the first missing person's case that was resolved by the spirit themselves. A true missing person – in Spirit.

Sam, the reporter, made me smile that day as she said she had been totally overwhelmed by witnessing every word that was expressed. She said she had never witnessed anything like this before. And it was her first big assignment, as she was relatively new to the job. It was over lunch when she almost apologetically asked if she, too, could have a sitting. In between the starter and the pudding, I was able to give her a loving communication from her beloved grandmother! It was from that day's events, after chatting to the photographer who arrived later, that I became a columnist for *Chat – It's Fate* magazine. What a fateful meeting it was indeed!

Tell the World

On 10th December, 2002, the first anniversary of my sister's death, I had a call from a *Kilroy* show researcher inviting me to be one of Kilroy-Silk's main guests on his TV show in London. I was invited to talk about my mediumship. It was my first television invitation. The invitation lifted my spirit because it coincided with the date and place of my sister's passing. So it was no surprise at all when the date for filming was scheduled a week later, on the exact anniversary of her cremation.

It was comforting in a way to think that her spirit had had a hand in it someway. I enjoyed the experience of the show, discussing my beliefs for the first time to such a wide audience, being asked questions – and even receiving the odd jibe or two – all in a very diplomatically controlled forum overseen by the charming and totally professional Robert Kilroy-Silk. I found him to be less of a sceptic than I'd initially expected, as at the end of the show he gave a very positive summary of someone's personal experience of mediumship.

'Telling the world about Spirit' was just unfolding, as I began to give people food for thought, touching millions with my 'gift' and knowledge of the Spirit World through the power of the media. And it was just about to expand on a greater scale.

I wasn't too sure, initially, about an invitation to the radio station Kerrang! to speak on Tim Shaw's late show. I will have had to be forgiven as I hadn't heard of Kerrang! or Tim before, but I said 'yes' all the same. They asked if I could be interviewed on the subject of 'psychic detective' work, as they had read in the press about the assistance I gave on a murder case.

I soon found out what the station was about! When I mentioned it to my son, he seemed surprised. He said he couldn't believe that I was going on a heavy-metal station! He was a little concerned, as he knows that that type of music isn't quite my cup of tea.

'Oh, well,' I said, 'I'll just tell them I've got Jimi Hendrix with me!' as I tried to flower things up with my usual sense of humour!

The evening soon arrived. I had spent hours, as usual, wondering what outfit to wear. I opted for a conservative look – a suit – which was my usual attire while working for Spirit. As I drove into Birmingham, I switched on the radio and tuned in to Kerrang! I became a bit apprehensive about being a guest when I heard a DJ advertising me as 'Angela Mc*Ghoulies*, a lady who can talk to the dead!' I began to question the intentions of the interview. I called the producer of the show and reminded her that I took my work very seriously and hoped that the interview would be of a similar nature. She reassured me it would be.

I couldn't help but smile when I arrived at the radio station: I thought those in the Spirit World were having a little laugh at my expense because, as I walked into the reception area, there, in your face and larger than life, was a portrait of none other than Jimi Hendrix himself! I laughed and began to relax as I entered the studio. I was surprised to see the DJ surrounded by an entourage of young people clad in black T-shirts and covered in piercings, while there was I in my suit! I felt a little bit like Mother Teresa sitting among them! Even the DJ remarked that I was the first colour-coordinated guest they'd ever had. I could believe it!

The interview went well. They all listened attentively – although I did notice a raised eyebrow or two as I talked in detail about the visions I had had at the scene of a crime.

I was then asked unexpectedly if I would do a reading live on air. I agreed. It was my first reading across the airwaves. I was a little bit nervous, but I had done telephone readings before to individuals some distance away. This time it was a little bit different as I would have large numbers of people listening in. As usual I just put all my trust and faith with those in Spirit to help me, Which they did, as I began to talk to a young man on the end of the line.

'I am being made aware that you have a grandfather in the Spirit World, on your father's side of the family.' I continued, 'My goodness! Your grandfather was a big man. The only way I can describe him is he's like a gentle giant,' I said.

The young man's voice stuttered nervously as he replied, 'Yes, I do have a grandfather who's passed over and he was a big man.'

'There is something about not one but two college courses you did not finish, so your grandfather is telling me.'

'I can't believe this,' he said, as he laughed nervously and admitted he had dropped out of two college courses!

I noticed the wide-eyed looks I was getting from the DJ and the young people surrounding him.

'Your grandfather wants you to finish your college studies. He also mentions the game of rugby. Do you play rugby?'

'Yes, I do,' he said

'I am being shown a watch. I believe you have a watch that belonged to your grandfather?'

'I do. You're absolutely amazing!' he added, as the pitch of his voice began to change as he became even more surprised.

It was a sheer pleasure to connect him with his grandfather. The point of his grandfather's message was to tell him to stop playing around and get on with his college course!

That evening was an education not only for me but for the young people there and listening in, too. It was an eye-opening experience. As I was leaving, I was reminded by the producer that the photograph they had taken of me would be put on the radio website, if I cared to look later.

It was a few days later that I logged on to the website for the first time. I remembered the DJ's comment about my colour-coordinated outfit as I looked at the photographs of his previous guests – who happened to be a string of semi-nude women and porn queens! To be the first colour-coordinated guest was an understatement – it seemed I was their first guest with clothes on! But a fascinating experience all in all.

I later appeared on the *Janice Long Show* on BBC radio to discuss my 'psychic detective' work. Janice had read about me in the press – I was getting quite a lot of nationwide coverage by then. I was acquiring nicknames such as 'the Midlands Psychic Detective' and 'the Miss Marple of the Spirit World'. A string of radio invitations followed. One particular radio invitation stemmed from my first theatre tour, which involved evenings appearing solo, telling stories and communicating messages from Spirit to an audience.

I was appearing at the Prince of Wales Theatre in Cannock. The theatre began to fill and I could hear the hustle and bustle of the audience from my dressing room. I had spent a couple of hours preparing myself for my new venture. I was about to appear before hundreds of people and it felt totally different from what I was used to. I had prayed that all my loved ones in Spirit would be there on that stage with me, helping me. I heard my introduction as I waited in the wings. I could feel the energies rise from the audience. It was powerful. Just as the curtains were beginning to open, I got a lovely surprise – I could see my sister's and my grandmother's spirits standing in the centre of the stage beckoning me on excitedly, as if they, too, couldn't wait. I felt like crying, but I braced myself and stepped forward.

There is always a tendency to remember the first and last messages as I go off on a high vibration of communication and become totally absorbed, instrumented by the Spirit and being somewhat in trance most of the evening. My first visitor from Spirit with a message was an Irish grandmother from County Galway, who wanted to connect with a lady in the front row. I pointed to the lady and asked her, 'Who's Peter?'

'That's him,' she said, pointing to the gentlemen sitting next to her.

'Who's Mary, then?' I said.

'That's me,' she replied. The audience chuckled at the alarmed way in which they looked at one another.

'It is obvious that your grandmother wants to speak to both of you, then,' I said. Her grandmother went on to confirm what she knew about their lives, although she had passed a few years before, but Spirit often does come through to confirm knowledge of recent events.

It was a show to remember, as it had a finale like no other. Just as I was saying goodnight and thanking the audience, as they began to applaud and I was walking off towards the wings, thinking my work for Spirit was over for the evening, I found myself turning round and rushing back to the centre of the stage. I was being called back by the pleas of a little boy's voice in Spirit saying, 'Please don't go! Please don't go!'

I glanced down and in between the aisles. I could see a little boy's spirit coming through, driving a yellow tractor. It was obvious he needed desperately to communicate. I surprised myself by saying, 'Please, please don't go just yet!' to the audience, as half of them were already standing, waiting to filter out.

'I have a young boy here who is desperate to communicate. There's a young boy on a yellow tractor and I am being made aware there is a lady here he wishes to communicate with, but I feel it is not his mother, though the lady is aware of his mother. He is trying his best to get a message through.'

The audience seemed to freeze, motionless. I pointed to a lady in a red coat. She said she knew him, as she acknowledged the little boy's plea. 'You must be a relative of some sort?' I said. She told me she was his aunt and that she would be seeing his mother the next day. I confirmed to her that the little boy had passed in an accident and that the yellow tractor was still kept in a garden shed, and that he had passed over to Spirit some years before. He wanted to send love to his mummy so much, and to tell her that he was all right now. And that he had met up with his grandmother in the Spirit World, who now looked after him.

'That's all he needs to say, so goodnight and God bless,' I said. The audience applauded yet again. This time I felt it was for the little boy, for he was the star of the show.

That show seemed to pass so quickly I couldn't even remember having received the cue from the technician to wind things up. I was convinced I had cut the show short in some way. I asked the technician, 'I finished that a little early, didn't I?'

'No love, you didn't. In fact you're half an hour late!' It just confirmed to me how much in trance I really was.

There was another surprise attached to that show, which I didn't find out till months later when I received an email from a BBC journalist called Jules McCarthy, who confessed to me that she was in the audience that evening and, to her utter surprise, she too had received a profound message from her beloved grandfather in Spirit. She was so impressed that she went back to BBC radio and recommended that they got me 'on air'.

It was shortly after that show I got invited to do a couple of guest slots on the *Keith Middleton Late Show* and also on his Saturday afternoon show. After that, he said he would like to find me a regular slot. He came up with the idea of me coming on the radio and making predictions before each of the England football matches during the World Cup.

That was a challenge I couldn't refuse! Keith had laid down the gauntlet. So I agreed to do it, although it meant putting my 'gift' to the test. But after all, my invitations to do radio work and be in the media were all destined to happen.

My first introduction began a week before the World Cup actually started. I was asked to make predictions about the warm-up match between England and Jamaica. I tried my best to educate Keith with regards to my gift and mediumship. I told him my gift was about helping the needy, not the greedy. It may or may not be the case that I would give the correct score each time, but if I did we would have half the betting nation in Britain running to the bookmakers, making lots of easy money! Life is not about that, and the gift is certainly not about that either. Besides, the Spirit World would want to prove its existence in some way during the process.

So, as we went live on air, I explained that I was sitting holding a photograph of my late grandfather, Jack Gavin, who had been a footballer in his day. I had said my prayers all week, asking him to come and give me some advice or knowledge – I desperately needed his help. Just as I had finished explaining, I heard my grandfather's voice in my ear. He was getting all excited, as he shouted, 'It's the big fella! It's the big fella!' He was referring to England's 6' 7" player, Peter Crouch. I then had a vision of Peter Crouch doing his celebratory robot dance, the one he would do back then after he scored. I turned to Keith and said, 'Keith, it's my granddad. He is referring to the "big fella", Peter Crouch. My prediction is we are going to see Peter Crouch do his robot dance time and time again during this match.'

With that statement fresh off my lips I came off air – and within minutes Peter Crouch had scored his first goal. One of three that day. What a hat trick, and what a triumph for the Spirit World!

The predictions I made relating to that match made the papers. But there was a greater prediction that proved true, word for word, in the weeks that followed. It was just before the England versus Ecuador match. I was ready to give my prediction across the airwaves when Keith cued me in saying, 'What insight have you got for England today, Angela?'

I replied instantly and without prior thought, saying, 'Today, Keith, David Beckham will score, England will win and Portugal will be our next opponent.' These unexpected words came out of my mouth like bullets. Or more like thoughts travelling at the speed of light.

Ninety minutes later, all that I predicted had come true: Beckham had scored, England had won and

Portugal had qualified to become England's next opponents!

I had to wait a week to hear Keith's response. Keith said he was 'spooked' by my predictions. He started my introduction by saying, 'Something really spooky happened last week!' He went on to explain to listeners about the results of my predictions. I was given a prerecorded round of applause.

'How did you know that?' Keith asked quizzically.

'By the speed of light, Keith, speed of light!' I said, keeping him more enraptured!

My predictions during the World Cup were overall successful – sadly more successful than England's bid!

Soon after this, I was contacted by a film producer who was making a documentary programme for Channel 4 about psychic children. She wanted to use my expertise and knowledge to assess a so-called psychic child, whom I would not actually meet. She wanted me to go to the child's home and meet the child's mother and further assess the situation by sensing psychically around the home, and in the process confirm to the child's mother what the child was experiencing or being a witness to. I wasn't even told whether the child was a boy or a girl.

Apparently the producer had already filmed a number of mediums who had felt could not get good enough results. The producer said they were relying on me, as their scheduled time for filming was running out.

Even though I was given no details, I didn't mind because I do sometimes prefer to work 'blind'. It helps not to confuse the thoughts from Spirit with known facts. I arrived on a housing estate in Birmingham where I met the crew and the child's mother, whose name was Jenny. She welcomed me as she answered the door. As I walked through the hallway, I instantly became very aware and drawn to the landing at the top of the stairs. I had planned first to walk around downstairs, so I kept my initial feelings under wraps until later. I spent several minutes walking around the living room. I sensed nothing at all, not even the slightest change in the energy field, but I was drawn to notice one of several different photographs of children hanging on the wall. I pointed to one of them. It was a photograph of a young boy about 10 years old.

'This is your son, the psychic child,' I said.

'Yes, he's the one,' said Jenny with a smile.

'I feel very drawn to go upstairs now, may

I?' 'Yes, feel free,' she answered.

I went upstairs and stood on the landing. I could feel a dramatic change in the temperature. It felt like I was standing in a vortex, a door to the Spirit World. I was aware of different energies passing through. I had a vision of her son running scared across the landing and I sensed a male spirit.

'Jenny,' I said, 'your son's sensitivity scares him at times, doesn't it? I sense he is aware of activity in this area here. I feel he would rather run across the landing than walk. I believe he asks often for the landing light to be kept on at night. Is that not so?' 'Yes he does, in fact,' she said.

'This here is like a door to the Spirit World. Your son sees the spirit of a man. This man is not known to him, but I sense he is an uncle of yours. I feel this uncle is your father's brother,' I said.

'Oh, my goodness! I do have an uncle who has passed over and my son has mentioned a man standing here!'

I pointed to the actual spot where the spirit had shown himself. I asked her if she noticed the change in temperature at times and explained that it can fluctuate to the extremes when Spirit is around. Also Spirit can create movement in the atmosphere, often like a light gust of wind brushing past. 'Which I feel your
son describes as someone brushing and touching his face?'

'Yes, he quite often does say that!' Jenny replied.

I felt very drawn to enter the young boy's bedroom where I sensed another visitor from Spirit, as for a couple of seconds I glimpsed a young boy standing there of a similar age to Jenny's son. He was wearing a navy blue pullover, a blue shirt and grey knee-length trousers. I described to Jenny what I could see. 'He has only just recently told me about the boy who comes and stands by his bed. In fact he stands exactly where you are standing now,' she said.

'He obviously looks like he lived in a different era, looking at his clothes,' I said.

'That's another strange thing, as the way my son describes him is as someone who wears "old" clothes.'

I went on to say that Jenny's son's sensitivity was not just confined to absorbing the energies found in the boundaries of their home. I then had a flashback to my own childhood. Spirit was bringing through a mutual psychic link, and so I continued to say, 'Your son not only sees Spirit here, but in other places. I am aware he senses Spirit children with him at school.'

'Yes, that's right. He has mentioned seeing them at school as well.'

I continued to talk to Jenny about her son's awareness and my own childhood psychic experiences. It was during this discussion that I started to link up with Jenny, as a lady from Spirit was wanting to communicate to her. Thus began an unexpected personal sitting as the lady began to communicate. It was Jenny's grandmother. She said she was very proud of Jenny and her college work and that it was going to lead her into the caring profession. Her grandmother also said not to get too frustrated with it as she would succeed. Jenny was shocked. She hadn't expected any message at all, but confirmed all I had said.

After this lovely interruption we discussed the bonuses and pitfalls of having a 'channel' in the family, and my advice was for her to continue to let her son talk about his experiences without putting any emphasis on the events. That she should let her child's gift evolve naturally without fear. I did not doubt that it would, as she has a truly psychic child.

The events of that day were similar to the work I did for a while for a particular 'psychic' company. I was hired as a medium to take tourists around historic places late at night, in the hope that we would discover and communicate with spirits from the past. This was indeed the case on numerous occasions, but my employers did not realize that we might not have only historic spirits coming through but in some cases the spirits of the tourists' loved ones as well! An added surprise to the event!

I made some wonderful discoveries in the halls, mansions and castles I visited during my evenings entertaining tourists. The story with Jenny's son shows that it is not necessarily the case, as some people think, that Spirit energy is more likely to be witnessed only in historic places and not in ordinary homes. It is wherever the spirit wishes to be acknowledged.

One particular discovery in an historic building gave us something we hadn't expected, but thinking about it later there was an obvious reason why. It was when BBCi – a local TV news programme for digital, satellite and Internet viewers – was first being launched. I was asked to do a piece to camera about my work. The setting was the historic Oak House in West Bromwich, which dates back to the 1600s.

It was late one evening in October when I was asked to tour the building to see if I could sense any spirit or activity and confirm who or what it was. I was met by a reporter who was geared up with film and sound equipment almost like a one-man band (or, in this case, a one-woman band!). I was then introduced to the curator and an historian. The historian was going to be used during filming to confirm and feed back any information or details I would receive through Spirit. The curator seemed very sceptical, and stated that it might be a case of me already knowing the history of the building, as it had been well publicized. In fact, I hadn't read about its history, although I was aware of the building.

I took on board what he said and asked my Spirit Guides to help sway this man. As they stood close by, and just as my mike was being pinned onto my lapel by the reporter, I instantly said to her, 'Denniston, in Glasgow.'

She almost squealed and dropped the microphone as she said, 'My family are from Denniston in Glasgow! That's amazing!'

I was beginning to sense that, although the historian seemed equally amazed, the curator looked surprised for a while but not convinced.

We began the tour. I sensed the spirit of a lady on the large staircase. It was confirmed that she was often seen by many people in the same place. I got a name that sounded like 'Burton' but in fact it was actually 'Turton'. I felt this lady was a member of a family that lived there many centuries ago. I also sensed the smell of fire. It was confirmed that there had been a fire at some time in the building's history. I continued sensing different energies.

The curator continued to follow us round and listened attentively with little or no expression on his face. Then all of a sudden I felt very drawn to look out of the window and onto the vast green lawns that were lit up by floodlights. I had a vision – I could 'see' that where the lawns were now situated there had stood an old black-and-white cottage-type building at one time. I turned to the historian and the curator and described what I could see. I also told them I sensed someone called Mr Baker, who was saying something about '25 years', but I felt this gentleman belonged to more recent times.

'My goodness!' said the historian, as she turned to the curator. 'That's Mr Baker, our old caretaker, who used to live in the cottage, which was pulled down and was situated out there, exactly where Angela is pointing. He was our caretaker for 25 years from the 1970s.'

She then changed her tone of voice and looked at the curator once again, aware of his scepticism, as she told him, 'Now then, that sort of information is *not* written up in the history of this building. It would be only in the employment records, and they're certainly not available to the public.'

The curator was left almost speechless! I felt as if I'd 'rested my case'! I left that evening, thanking everyone, including my Spirit Guides.

My biggest audience was yet to come. Through the combination of the power of Spirit and the media, I am able to 'tell the world about Spirit' just as was prophesied all those years ago. Everything came together when I made a documentary about my 'psychic detective' work as part of a series called *Psychic Investigators*. This series is about crimes that are solved through a combination of detective work and the paranormal power of a psychic. The programme challenges sceptics to explain the inexplicable and, for believers, it confirms a mysterious world beyond observable fact.

Psychic Investigators has now been shown in more than 80 countries around the world. My God! I really am 'telling the world' – and I hope I continue to do so.

As a result of the series I was given a regular radio slot in the US on a programme called *The Afterlife Show*. This was another challenge, as each week I would bring communication from loved ones in Spirit to individuals in the US, recorded live from my home here in England via the radio waves, the Spirit World and the power of the latest technology. It proves there is no such thing as 'distance' with Spirit, as it is a fact that the power of Spirit is beyond the universe.

It was, for me, a new and different way of working with Spirit, but all the same allowed me to continue to bring comfort and, ultimately, proof to people that their loved ones are not 'lost', that their loved ones can communicate across the globe. Even on live radio!

And the little ex-convent girl from Liverpool is left feeling very humbled by it all.

Angels, Heroes, Saints and Sinners

Cherub

I was looking forward to attending a friend's birthday party at the weekend, but as I was waking up on the Friday before, I heard my Guide say that my daughter would be having her baby that weekend. It was to be my first grandchild. I found myself phoning my friend telling her the reason I wouldn't be at the party. She was used to my ways by now. I had still had to break the news to my daughter – that she should prepare herself for the delivery. When I called to tell her what I had heard, she was quite anxious. She didn't feel prepared and a part of her didn't want to believe it was really going to happen. 'It can't happen this weekend,' she said. 'I've got three more antenatal check-ups to go to. The baby's not due for another two weeks. Anyway, I've got a check-up this afternoon. I'll see what the midwife has to say.'

That afternoon she returned from her antenatal check-up almost in tears. She began to explain that the midwife had said she had recently noticed that there had been a discrepancy about the expected due dates at the beginning of my daughter's pregnancy. The doctor had now decided to go with the first given dates, which would make the pregnancy now 10 days overdue, and that would mean she would be admitted into hospital the very next day, Saturday, for an induced delivery.

We arrived with bags in hand early the next day. I hoped I was wrong – the thought of a long labour was harrowing – but I kept quiet about what I was sensing.

The day certainly seemed long. She was moved from one ward to another as she waited for her labour to begin. I sat beside her preparing myself for a long wait. This is where we met up with two other expectant young mothers, who seemed to be having 'trouble' during their pregnancies. They chatted with us to help break the boredom.

One of the young mothers shared her excitement with us by saying that she knew she was having a boy. My daughter asked if she'd had a scan to decipher the sex, as she appeared to be fairly early on in her pregnancy.

'No, no,' she said. 'I haven't had a scan. I know because a medium told me. I am having a boy.'

My daughter turned to me and grinned. Before I could say, 'Let's be a little discreet here,' she blurted out, 'Oh! My mum's one of them.' The two expectant mothers' eyes seemed to light up, as they sat up to attention in their beds.

My daughter begged, 'Please, Mum, go on, tell them something. It's boring here waiting.'

She would often treat my gift like a party piece. But I didn't mind. I felt obliged, as usual.

I just wanted something light-hearted to say to cheer them up, as they stared at me like I was some kind of magician ready to perform my next trick.

I began to 'sense' and said to one of them, 'I can "see" a pet shop round you. And that you have a grandfather who has passed over, who used to have a large Alsatian dog, I believe?'

'My goodness,' she said, looking pleasantly surprised. 'I own a pet shop, and my grandfather *did* have an Alsatian. It's nice to know that he has his Alsatian with him now.'

I felt I had to go over to the other expectant mother and say something discreetly to her. I went over to her bed. Without prior thought, I said, 'I know you are here for obvious reasons, but I "sense" there is something there inside you, alongside the baby.' I knew I had to say it for a reason. It was obvious to me that her Guides had influenced my thoughts. As I continued, she sat with her mouth wide open for a while, then she explained, 'Doctors have just told me that I have fibroids growing with the baby. However did you know that?'

'Because you have a grandmother in Spirit on your mother's side of the family who has not long passed over. She is watching over you and she says that you and the baby will be fine.' I held her hand. She smiled at me with tears in eyes. Placing her hand on mine and, with a sigh of relief, she said, 'Thank you.'

Just then there was a welcome interruption. A nurse arrived to take my daughter to the delivery ward. In the hours that followed, my daughter's labour pains began to take hold. The midwife seemed to be fascinated by what I did for a living, and she asked me a lot of questions. She explained that 'whispers' had gone around the hospital like wildfire about there being a renowned psychic expecting her first grandchild on the wards. The whispers were obviously started by the young expectant mothers I'd given messages to.

This time my daughter was not impressed with the subject of mediumship being bandied about. She screamed at the midwife in the midst of her pains, reminding the midwife that she was about to give birth and that the midwife should be concentrating on her. She was a bit rude, but the midwife was forgiving as she said she was used to young mums in pain and under the influence of gas and air.

It got to quarter to midnight and the midwife announced, 'One more push and the baby will be here before midnight.' I stood alongside my daughter and her partner, doing everything I could to help encourage her to make that final push, as she was becoming exhausted.

I then became aware of a presence. I smelled a perfumed aroma around me and sensed it was my grandmother Kathleen. I heard her say, 'No! 2.35.' I found myself repeating these words and saying out loud, 'No! 2.35.'

The midwife glared at me. She must have thought 'how rude' to go against her professional judgement. The midwife piped up and said, 'No! Take no notice of your mum, one more push and the baby *will* be here before midnight.'

I didn't mean to sound obnoxious or undermine her professional judgement. My grandmother must have known that we would worry about the length of time it was taking.

As it turned out, the baby got stuck in the birth canal – but thankfully, finally arrived, looking like a little cherub, pure and perfect. My daughter, her partner and I were too in awe of the baby to notice the midwife glancing over at the clock. She looked shocked. I looked up and saw that it was 2.35 a.m.

I grinned, but I was more engrossed with the emotions surrounding my beautiful baby granddaughter, as I became aware of my loved ones in Spirit arriving to take a glance at the newborn spirit who had just arrived on Earth. I saw my grandmother Kathleen standing beside the bed, smiling down at the newborn wonder. She lifted her head and said, 'She, too, will be blessed.' I was engrossed in my thoughts as they were interrupted by the midwife as she passed me the baby to hold, while she tended to my daughter. I held her and just knew she was special.

The midwife then took the baby back from me, to weigh her. I smiled at the midwife and said, 'Six pounds, twelve ounces'. Again, I had been listening to my grandmother's words.

The midwife said, 'I'm finding this unbelievable,' as she turned round. 'She's six pounds, twelve ounces.' She said it in a frustrated tone, as if she wanted to rationalize things in her own mind but couldn't.

I just shrugged, almost apologetically, and got on with tending the other little miracle in my life, my beautiful granddaughter.

My grandmother waved to me, her 'signature' wave, and disappeared once more. I understood that I had now been blessed with yet another gifted child in the family.

The whispers around the wards continued in the weeks that followed, and as a result I was inundated with calls and visits from hospital staff.

Our loved ones visit us not only when we are grieving and to help our loved ones cross over but also at joyful times when we are celebrating.

As for my granddaughter, she was given the name of Kathleen, after her great-great-grandmother. As she got older, she expressed on numerous occasions her sensitivity to Spirit, as gifted children often do and as I did as a child. My daughter and I understand it when others don't, and embrace it. We knew, for instance, that she was having a spiritual experience when she first described her visits at night by the 'sparkling lights'. And the little boy she talked about and played with. We both knew it was not her 'imaginary friend' but a child from the Spirit World.

Confirmation came when she was five years old, when one night it was arranged for her to stay at my house. My son and I were sat watching TV when we heard the scurrying of little feet running down the stairs and into the living room. She could hardly catch her breath; she was excited as she said, 'Nanny, there is a lady and two little girls upstairs.' 'Yes! Yes,' I said, as I had sensed this lady and the two little girls a few years before, when I'd first moved into the house. I was so excited and proud of my granddaughter. The thought that she could actually 'see' Spirit was humbling. I reassured her and said as calmly as I could, 'Yes, honey, it's OK, they're Nanny's friends, they only want to say hello to you,' and I gave her a big hug.

Weeks later on one of her visits, I found myself wondering if she had received anything else as she wandered around the rooms of the house. As she sat eating her dinner, I asked her if she had seen any of 'Nanny's friends' lately. To my surprise, she said, 'Yes, Nanny.'

'Oh really?' I said casually. 'What were they doing?'

'They were clapping hands and tickling me,' she said.

'Did they speak to you?' I asked. I wanted to know if she could hear them.

'Yes,' she replied. 'They said, "Thank you for telling Nanny."'

I almost choked on my food. I stroked her hair and patted her head. That just summed it all up. She was able to see and hear and relay a message. Bless her.

These familiar 'friends' of mine had first become apparent to me when I moved into the property. First I became aware of strange noises I would often hear at night. Some I could fathom out to be the pitter-patter of small feet, so I sensed there was more than one child. One particular noise was strange and I couldn't fathom it out. It was like metal grinding and knocking.

The girls would often appear in my dreams. In the daytime hours I would often hear them calling out for their mummy.

Their mummy was a very busy person, so I found out one day. It was when a group of Jehovah's Witnesses were on their 'rounds'. They came down the street knocking on all the doors. Jehovah's Witnesses were people I would often chat to, and I did that day as usual. A member of their group happened to be an elderly lady. After she stood there and listened to the conversation we'd had about our individual beliefs, she randomly told me she used to visit my house as a small child because the local seamstress once lived there and the lady had made her one of her very first winter coats. She added she used to work day and night at her sewing machine. It was then I knew what the strange noise was: the pedal of her old wrought-iron sewing machine.

I thought it wonderful all the same, that the gift in my family had now been passed down to a future generation. I hope in time she will embrace the greater sense of spirituality for years to come.

Nell

My great-aunt Nell was a spinster. She stood just under five feet tall. She may have been small in stature but she was mighty in spirit. Her spirit graced this Earth plane for more than 95 years. She had a warm sense of Liverpudlian humour and was a woman of great faith, the most devout Catholic anyone could meet. You didn't have to be a medium to sense the warmth of her spirit. She used to tell me stories of when she was a little girl, going back to the turn of the century, and of how she used to get into trouble for sneaking away from her father's blacksmith forge to run, free-spirited, through the cobblestoned streets of the city, running down to the dock to see the big ships coming in and watch them offload their valuable cargos. It all sounded like another world to me.

Auntie Nell was not only well respected and loved by all of her large extended family but also by those people whose presence she graced, as she always left you with a positive impression. She commanded great reverence and earned herself the title of 'Auntie Nell' to all who knew her. She also helped to raise many a needy child, in particular the ones she took under her wing during wartime. I don't suppose she ever really missed out on motherhood. She was very well known in her local community and church for her fundraising efforts and the help she gave people in their daily lives.

Auntie Nell Uriell

She became somewhat 'iconic' – even the Bishop of Liverpool graced her presence once when he came to tea, an event at which she insisted that everyone should call her Auntie Nell, even the bishop! She explained that that was her 'title' and that was what people called her, even those who were not related to her.

The most fitting words people would use to describe her were 'Angel' or 'Saint'. I couldn't argue with that, for it was true. What confirmed this for me was when I learned – and was amazed and delighted to do so – that her full name was Ellen Uriell. Uriel is a biblical archangel. The name just suited the whole sense of her spiritual being.

Nell was the one woman I turned to when I was ill and asked her to light a candle for me and say a prayer, which she did. I was aware of her healing nature, even if she was not. She gave me an answer when one day she handed me a glass card with words engraved on the glass that expressed her sentiments and thoughts, and the answer to the prayer. I am convinced that it was her healing thoughts and prayers that helped to cure me.

Auntie Nell became blind in the last years of her life. It was something she just came to terms with and accepted almost naturally. She would often crack jokes about her own disabilities; nothing seemed to deter her – and her mission – in any way. One of the last efforts

P. & E. URIELL,
HAME & CHAIN MAKERS,
HANDCARTS & TRUCKS REPAIRED,
14, HEAD STREET, PARK PLACE,
Residence—29, GT. NEWTON STREET,

Liverpool.

General Blacksmiths. All Orders promptly attended to.

Auntie Nell and Bishop

she made on behalf of others was when she became one of the oldest people to take part in a charity 'bed push'. She lay in a makeshift hospital bed while students pushed her through the streets of Liverpool city centre – to her sheer delight – in aid of raising funds for a local children's hospital.

Nell passed over in September 1996 and went back home to the Realm of Spirit, shortly after her 95th birthday. I was unable to attend her funeral, but I was told that the priest paid a fitting tribute to her by saying, 'Little did we know that we had a saint in our midst.' She would have smiled down upon us at that point and tittered in delight, sharing the same sentiments as myself. 'Saint Nellie of Liverpool' has not got the same ring somehow, for me and for many others, as our 'angel', Auntie Nell.

The day of her funeral, my son was in hospital and I found I needed her help, God's help – anyone's help – more than ever in my life. My son had collapsed as a result of some kind of brain seizure. The doctors told me he was seriously ill and that he would have to undergo tests. The function of his brain had broken down and he couldn't communicate or function properly. I would have given anything to have taken his place that day. He was just 18 years old. His life hung in the balance. I felt so helpless and fearful and I never felt so alone in all of my days. Where was God in all of this? I questioned. I knew He was somewhere in the equation, but I could not feel anyone's presence, as I begged, prayed and pleaded for help. I was in a state of shock that lasted for months, but I still had to function and, again, as usual, be 'everything to everyone'.

I sat beside him practically from morning till night in the first few months of his illness. One evening while he was sleeping, I placed a set of rosary beads above his bed. It was the set that Auntie Nell had bought him for his Holy Communion. Each evening as I left him, I would ask Auntie Nell to watch over him until the next morning while I was home looking after the rest of the family.

Months went by. I never felt so alone in my anguish. The hospital corridor seemed to be getting longer and longer each day. It was a daunting time. It felt like my soul was becoming detached from my body. I was struggling with the pretence that I was coping. Inside I was dying; the emotional pain was crippling me. There was so much I had bottled up inside, not just the pain of my son's tragedy. It was all the emotional pain I'd ever felt, churning up inside me.

In these darkest moments, there came a glimmer of hope as my son spoke his first words sentence for several months. He said, 'Mum, all I've dreamt about is Auntie Nell.'

I broke down and sobbed uncontrollably, like that small convent child all over again. I knew Auntie Nell had been watching over him and I hadn't been alone. My son had not seen his Auntie Nell since his Holy Communion 10 years before and he wasn't aware that she had recently passed over. It was obvious God had sent her.

During that period when I felt so deserted, I also began to realize that the Spirit World was trying its best to get through to me in a message which presented itself in the words of a particular song. This song had an uncanny way of interrupting my day. I would hear it playing in unusual places and it would crop up with perfect timing at poignant times. It seemed that no matter what time of day or night I left the hospital, it would be the first song I would hear on the car radio. God and my loved ones were doing their best to contact me. I didn't realize, although I was demanding that they come and help, that I was set too deeply in my emotions and had put up barriers to my 'sensitivity'.

The lyrics in question were from the Michael Jackson song 'You Are Not Alone', and they just said it all for me: 'You are not alone. I am here with you.' It was no coincidence that I kept hearing these words everywhere I went. It is a way in which Spirit can communicate their presence. I realize that I am – and we are – never alone. That one song is among others that have presented themselves in this way to me over the years, and each one has left a mark on my soul.

In the 10 long years since that time, my son has made progress, although he has been left with a vulnerability. I have never been so proud of him as I am today for what he has had to endure and the bravery he has shown in the process. He has become very philosophical about the whole experience. I have two sons: one has had all the 'glory' of being a footballer, the other has had all the pain. How diverse can two pathways be? It just goes to show that each and every one of us is on our very own individual journey through life.

There is no greater pain than that of a mother's, so people say. The hardest thing to learn and accept is that, no matter how hard we try to guide and protect our children, our children are on their own individual pathways.

George

Some people are surprised, sometimes, when you bring through a communication from a relative they have never met. Our loved ones, no matter where they are in the history of our family, will often communicate with us. My great uncle, George Frederick Griffin, was one such soul whom I had never met but who certainly knew of me. And the message I received from him came as a lovely and unexpected surprise.

George Frederick Griffin was also known as 'Tim'. He was born on 3rd February, 1883, in Liverpool. He became one of the finest horsemen in history and he served in Queen Mary's own Hussars, where he was made sergeant in 1912. He was also encouraged to join the North West Mounted Police at Regina in Canada in August 1912 as a Riding and Foot Drill Inspector. He was rapidly promoted though the ranks to Sergeant Major and on 1st April, 1914, took charge of the horse-training school. One of his duties was choosing suitable horses. He selected all black horses – all fine-looking and welltrained animals – and formed the world-famous 'Musical Ride', in which he was the master riding instructor in charge. His horses were chosen to escort King George VI and Queen Elizabeth's visit in 1939 – marking the first occasion when an all-black horse-mounted escort was used, and setting a precedent for the future.

In the spring of 1940, George was sent out to Hollywood to drill the actors who would represent the North West Mounted Police in Cecil B. DeMille's film, *North West Mounted Police* starring Gary Cooper and Preston Foster. It was a film that was nominated for a number of Oscars. How proud we all were to have such a person in the family.

Growing up I often read the newspaper cuttings of great-uncle George's adventures, and I remember the family being gathered round the old black-and-white TV, waiting for the thrill of seeing his name in the credits at the end of the film. We would do this each time it was shown, but it was a long wait between repeats in those days!

It was something else I kept quiet about as a child, as you could not tell people that your uncle had made a film with Gary Cooper. It would have been as unbelievable to most people as if I had said that I had had a visit from my dead grandmother!

Nowadays I am often asked by people why I have a photograph of a 'Mountie' on my living-room wall. I tell them with pride that he is my famous uncle who I am proud to have in my family. Another reason he takes pride of place is to remind me of the wonderful message he gave me through another medium. I had no intention of seeing another medium until my friend Linda phoned me one day to say that she had overheard two 'old dears' talking on the bus that morning and mentioning that there was 'a big psychic' coming to the local town hall. Instantly I received a picture in my mind and said to Linda, 'I know who it is, it's Stephen O'Brien.' As I said this, an image flashed up in my head of a poster I had seen of him on a noticeboard in a Spiritualist church a couple of years before. I explained that I felt I must have been given this vision for a purpose. I summed up by saying, 'We're going to buy tickets to see him, because that man has a message for me.'

Linda, slight sceptic that she was, dismissed it by saying, 'Don't be silly, there will be a few hundred people there at least. Who says he's going to talk to you?' 'I do,' I said.

And who do you think Stephen O'Brien picked out of the audience that evening, leaving Linda aghast? None other than myself! I was left totally warmed by his message as I was told something good was going to happen. Stephen O'Brien connected with me, as he sensed I worked for Spirit, and thanked me for my work. He then said he had a message from an Uncle George who had emigrated to Canada many years ago. Stephen stated that I'd never met him, but the reason

Uncle George was coming through was the connection with Canada. Uncle George said I was going to do some work with Spirit that connected with his beloved adopted country, Canada, and when it happened I would know for sure that Uncle George's spirit had had an influence in the process.

Sometimes when messages are given they can unfold in a matter of days or weeks, but others can take months or even several years to unfold. My understanding is that you are sometimes given a specific date or time, but at other times events simply unfold in their own time.

So it was several years later before I realized exactly what Uncle George's message had meant. It was when I filmed the documentary series *Psychic Investigators* about my work with the West Midlands police over the murder of Mick Hughes – with the Canadian film company Cineflix. But the 'punchline' came when I was given the contact name in Canada to forward my invoice to. It was to be forwarded to someone with the surname of none other than 'Griffin'. George was just confirming his influence!

Sgt Major. George Frederick Griffin

Oh Lord!

I was never so surprised as when I saw a gentleman who was dressed like a tin soldier, without the hat, standing at the foot of my bed one night. His presence woke me. I was confused and bewildered as I couldn't figure out who or what he was. I could see him in fine detail – he had a receding hairline and a bushy moustache, and wore some kind of period military costume with thick braiding and epaulettes. This rather regal figure stood in front of me and seemed to linger for more seconds than the usual 'visit', but he did not speak a word. Then he just disappeared.

I couldn't remember seeing anyone like that in any of my family albums, but I sensed he was connected in some way and that he had 'showed' himself for a reason. I was fascinated by him – and thankfully I didn't have to wait long to find out exactly who he was. It was a few days later when I was paying a visit to my Auntie Joan. She told me she had found a book in the local library which mentioned her sister, who had had a fairytale romance and had married a lord – Lord French, 3rd Earl of Ypres – back in 1972. I first heard about their marriage while I was in my early teens. It was rather grand to think that I was the niece to Lord and Lady French, but we lived cities – and worlds – apart. The only thing that connected us was the fact that their daughter and I shared the same middle name of Kathleen, as we were both named after our grandmother, Kathleen Murphy.

Auntie Joan showed me the book and there he was, the man I'd seen standing in my bedroom a few nights before. It turned out to be the 1st Earl, Lord French's grandfather. I explained this to my Auntie Joan. She seemed amazed as I told her about his 'visit'. We laughed about the fact that he hadn't spoken, as I said maybe it was because I wasn't regal enough for him to talk to me! We both agreed that he had come for a purpose.

Sometimes our loved ones just show themselves to let us know that they are walking alongside us. It may be a case that they come to say that they will be back shortly after to help a member of the family 'cross over' to the Other Side, or it could be because there is something major in our lives just about to happen and they want us to know that they are helping us by staying close and being aware of our endeavours.

DEBRETT'S ILLUSTRATED PEERAGE

YPRES, EARL OF (French)
(Earl UK 1922)

JOHN RICHARD CHARLES LAMBART FRENCH, 3rd Earl; b 30 Dec 1921; s 1958; ed Winchester, and at Trin Coll, Dublin European War 1939-45 as Capt King's Roy Rifle Corps; m 1st 1943 (m diss 1972), Maureen Helena, da of H John Kelly, US Foreign Ser (ret); 2ndly, 1972, Deborah, da of R Roberts of Liverpool, and has issue by 1st and 2nd m.

Arms – Ermine, a chevron sable, a crescent for difference. Crest – a dolphin embowed proper. Supporters – Dexter, a lion guardant & supporting a staff proper with a banner of the Union; sinister, a lion supporting a staff proper with a banner paly of three, sable, gold and gules.

DAUGHTERS LIVING

(By 1st marriage)

Lady Charlene Mary Olivia, b 1946: m 1983, Charles Mordaunt Milnes, son Milnet, Bt.
Lady Sarah Mary Essex, b 1963.
Lady Emma Mary Helena, b 1968: m 1980, Charles Geoffrey Humfrey, son of Charles Michael Humfrey, of Alderney, CI.

(By 2nd marriage)

Lady Lady Kathleen, b 1976.

I would rather die than be dishonoured.

It was a couple of weeks later I heard the news that my other auntie, Lady French, had had a massive stroke. The vision I'd had was all about the fact that her loved ones knew something was going to happen, and, most of all, that her late husband and his relatives were drawing close to her and were aware of her condition as they continued to walk beside her.

LINDA

It was November 1995 when I sensed strongly that there was something dreadfully wrong with Linda McCartney. I 'felt' she had received some bad news about her health. I mentioned this during a telephone conversation with a friend who I knew was a great Beatle fan, although we hadn't been discussing anything even slightly connected to them during the call. I said we were going to hear about Linda's health, and I explained that I felt that there was going to be a great loss for Paul. My friend refused to believe it, as she said that Linda was probably healthier than the two of us put together, considering her vegetarianism. But a few weeks later it was announced in the press that Linda had breast cancer.

Shortly after her passing, I received a totally unexpected communication from her, one which it took

Linda McCartney and me

me several years to find the appropriate time and place to pass on. There is no message that doesn't get to its destination, although some may take time.

Spirit takes so much energy and effort to produce a communication that none is wasted and it never fails to reach its destination. First Spirit will choose a 'channel' of their choice, a place and a time. It may be someone they have had a psychic link with or whom they know and who is a strong communicator. In my case I felt that she used me as her instrument because our souls had touched all those years before when we'd met on a number of occasions in the 1970s.

I am as sceptical as the next person when I hear of mediums channelling no one but famous people. But it all made sense, her coming to me, as we had already connected in this life.

Nevertheless, I would never have envisaged the circumstances which led to our meeting again – this time in Spirit. I was having what some people call a 'near-death experience' at the time. It all came about when I was rushed to hospital due to an allergic reaction. My body was going into anaphylactic shock. There were red weal-like marks surfacing on my skin. My temperature was high and my head, hands and feet were very swollen – to such a degree that I became unrecognizable.

I was feeling very lethargic and detached, as if I were conscious of my own spirit. It seemed like it was hovering, leaving my body.

My usual feelings would be that I would sense spirits' presence around me, as they had visited me many times before in hospital situations. And I often joked that I'd had that many operations that I was going to the Spirit World a bit at a time! This time it was different, though – I felt a sensation which seemed like my spirit leaving me through the top of my head. But I could still see myself. I saw and felt myself travelling towards a bright, piercing light. I then found myself lying down in a room full of light, surrounded by my loved ones who had crossed over. I heard a male voice tell me that it wasn't my time, and that I had to go back as there was work to do. I was conscious of my physical body being held down, but also conscious of my spirit body up on another dimension. I continued to travel until it seemed I had arrived in a beautiful garden, where I met up with Auntie Nell. She was smiling at me and sitting on a bench. I sat down beside her. She, too, told me I had to go back.

It was then, all of a sudden, that I saw Linda McCartney. She looked beautiful, dressed in blue. Her hair was long and pinned back on one side with a tropical flower. She came and sat beside me and chatted to me. It was then I became conscious again of my physical body and relayed what I had seen and heard to my friend who was sitting beside my bed. I drifted off again to the Realms of Spirit and listened and relayed over and over again what my loved ones and Linda had to say. She spoke of her passing and told me her ashes had been spread in two of her favourite places: the Mull of Kintyre and a place in Arizona where she had many of her fondest family memories. She spoke of her children and the love she wished to convey to them. She mentioned a favourite piece of pottery and a basket of dried wild flowers which hung in her kitchen. She spoke of her daughter, Stella, and said that she would get married on the Mull of Kintyre and that she, Linda, would be present. She also mentioned that Paul would remarry quickly, and this would be to a strong Northern woman. She seemed a little concerned when she mentioned this and her son James, but most of all she wanted to let Paul know that all was well with her. She wanted to convey all her love and to let them know that she was watching over them all.

My experience of my soul travelling at the speed of light did not stop there. It was during that same experience that I witnessed an Angel. It was larger than life and appeared at a time when my friend was convinced I was slightly delirious due to my high temperature, but up until that point she had had no doubts about the other spirits I had seen and mentioned. I was in a semiconscious state, but I had no doubt of what I saw. The sheer size of the angel stretched almost the entire height of the wall and across the ceiling of the hospital ward. I do not profess that the angel spoke to me, but the sight induced a beautiful feeling and a knowing that all was going to be well. After all, I had a mission of work to do, as my loved ones had told me.

It was several weeks before the swelling went and I was feeling ready to carry on my work for Spirit. But it was a puzzle to me how I was going to relay Linda's message, as decades had passed since our last meeting and I was now living at the other end of the country and had no connection whatsoever. But I knew that somehow and in some way Linda's message would finally filter through in good time.

It was a few years later when I thought my opportunity had come to pass. It was during a young lady called Stephanie's sitting, when I sensed that she had had a horrific accident 18 months previously, which had changed her life dramatically. She confessed to me that she had lost the bottom part of her leg, which was not obvious to see at that time as the injury was covered by her trousers. During her sitting, I told her I could 'see' her going into the teaching profession. She confirmed to me that she had plans to do just that. It was then that I began to think of Paul McCartney's new wife, Heather Mills. I used her as an example of someone who just got on with life in spite of her disability. When I mentioned Heather to her, Stephanie told me that Heather had in fact phoned her personally around the time she had had her accident, with words of hope and encouragement. She said that Heather would make it her business to find out about new and young amputees and contact them, which I thought was very admirable of her. For a split second I thought maybe Stephanie would be my link to pass on Linda's message, but I suppose it would have been totally inappropriate to tell a new wife that her husband's deceased wife wished to communicate from the Other Side. I still knew that one day soon I would release the message to wherever it was truly meant to go.

Again I thought of Linda's message a couple of years later when I paid a visit to a lady who lived in a very old converted barn. She had called me in to see what I could sense about her newly converted dwellings. Instantly I'd sensed she had a father in the Spirit World who had worked in the construction industry and who said that she was living his dream, as he had always wanted to one day convert his own barn. The lady wasn't expecting a message from her father, but she was so delighted when I told her that his spirit had had a hand in bidding for the property. She regarded it as a stroke of luck when she'd bought the property, as the two other people involved in the bidding had dropped out at the last minute. She was touched by the thought that her father had helped in this. I then sensed a historical connection with the barn, which confirmed the stories she had been told.

Later, after I had finished my communication, she began to ask me more general questions about my gift. One of them was if I had ever channelled anyone famous? With that question I remembered Linda, of course, and told her of her communication. This woman then said, 'How strange! My husband's construction company is just now doing work on Stella McCartney's new home in Worcester!' Again I thought, 'Is this a way through for Linda's message?' So I kindly asked, if her husband ever got into any conversation with Stella, could he drop a subtle hint about Linda's message in some way? But that never happened.

Finally the most appropriate time to release Linda's message of hope came, when I had almost forgotten it. It was only last year when I was being interviewed by a reporter from the *Liverpool Echo* about my life and work. We got to the end of the interview when the final question was, 'Have you ever had a message from anyone famous?' I thought the interviewer would be half-expecting me to say John Lennon. She was surprised when I told her about Linda. In fact it was me who was surprised, as the story made front-page news in the last week of August, when each year the city celebrates the Beatles. It was meant to be that Linda's message was to be released first in Liverpool, as it was a place she held dear, and at a time when it would reach not just visiting Beatle fans but, most of all, family and friends who still reside there.

OZZY- EPILOGUE

In December 2003 a familiar thing happened one morning while I was going about my daily chores. I was standing at the kitchen sink listening to music on the radio. A vision interrupted my thoughts – it was a picture of a couple standing either side of a man with long hair. It became clear it was Mr and Mrs Osbourne, Ozzy's parents, a couple who I had not given a thought to for over 30 years, but they had interrupted my sleep the night before with the same vision. I realized then that they must have both passed over. In the vision they were standing either side of someone I assumed was Ozzy's brother Tony, for he and Ozzy were hard to tell apart as they looked so similar, and Tony was the one

I'd been connected with all those years ago. I felt that Mr and Mrs Osbourne were watching over him for a purpose – maybe he was ill, I thought, or maybe something was about to happen. They came with a feeling of overpowering love, as if they stood there either side of him, protecting him.

The vision flashed up in my head time and time again that day. It left me with an over-powering urge to make contact in some way, but I also felt I would have to find a subtle way.

I had heard through the grapevine that Ozzy's brother still lived in the local area somewhere, so I went to the local library and looked him up on the electoral register where I found his address. I decided I was going to write him a letter – but as a reputable professional medium and not an ex-girlfriend, in the hope that the message would have more impact. I felt I needed to tell him that his parents where drawing close for a purpose. I wasn't sure what his parents' first names were, but all the same I had to pass on what I had seen in the recurring vision and make their contact known in some way. I felt it was the least I could do.

Everything I saw in that vision became more apparent a week or so later. I had been mistaken – it wasn't Tony they were standing alongside, it was Ozzy himself, as a week or so after the vision Ozzy suffered his near-fatal quad bike accident. I have no doubt that Mr and Mrs Osbourne were protecting him that day, and I am sure that Ozzy would agree.

In the process of time my 'visions' regarding Tony and his famous brother took me to a far deeper understanding of them, the previous events and the 'need' and purpose for on-going spiritual connections.

It was after the publication of my first book I made a conscious decision to give a copy of book to those signicant individuals and families that have played a part in my spiritual journey.

The 'Osbourne' family, particularly Tony, being part of it, was included on my list. But for many a good reason it took time to happen. It was almost a year in fact, that I had been meaning to deliver by hand, a copy of the book.

To my knowledge, he still lived in the local borough, so I'd heard.

But that event took a back burner due to my travelling further afield, promoting my book and working extensively with spirit. It was those people of the spirit world, as usual, who can draw my attention any time, using many different 'guises and timing'or when the timing of 'universal energy' saw fit.

So a scheduled sitting with a long haired man named Neil took place the day before a long awaited planned break

.

He arrived with a big beaming smile, a pleasant character, so he was. His Grandmother in spirit, seemed eager to connect to him, as I told him of her instant presence and said that he was the 'Apple of her eye'.so I could hear her say. She seemed so proud of him. The communication continued.

'She tells me you have a wonderful job, that takes you all over the world and it's all to do with music?' Is it not?

He didn't give a precise answer . He just laughed and said

'How do you know that?

'Your lovely grandmother tells me so' I replied

Then I heard ...

' Aah ! but he can't play a note'.

I relayed what she had said. I looked at him for an answer once again.

"My nan always spoke in riddles but yes she's right' he said ....it is all to do with music and I do travel the world but I am what you call a 'Roadie' that works along with Famous Bands and Artistes helping with transport, erecting equipment and more often seeing to their personnel needs, whilst 'on the road'. It's great. I get to see many a 'Star' and the world. I've been with one particular band for over twenty years now. We've become like mates. I'm off on tour again soon with them, as they are doing a 'revival' tour"

.

"Oh yes, which Band is that ? I asked, interrupting

.

He seemed surprised that a woman of my calibre would ask such detail as I 'sensed ' he thought It was irrelevant or immaterial or just not my taste.

"Er ….Black Sabbath". Came the reply.
(There it was, my hidden reminder, this meeting was by no coincidence It seemed, the planned days ahead had a purpose. I promised those in spirit I would deliver my book to Tony, the very next day).

'Now that doesn't surprise me' I said.
He then looked puzzled.
I went on to explain my connections and that he in a way, had been sent to me, not only for his purpose and that of his Grandmothers but mine too. After a long 'chat' with his 'Nan' and an insight to a glimpse of his future he left feeling content.
Little did I know that the spirit world would use him again in a 'timely' visit in the future, where he, himself would become the ' messenger.' for a famous friend.

The very next day I found myself standing outside the door at the only address I found locally, on the electrol register that seemed to fit Tony's circumstances as it stated he was living with a partner named Carole, so it fitted into place, to what I had already heard.
.

It was Carole that answered the door, as I quickly and somewhat nervously reeled off my 'rehearsed' introduction.

"Excuse me but does a Tony Osbourne live here, as I am a local Medium, who has wrote a book and I have mentioned him in it and I thought It was only polite to give him a copy.

' I took breathe, to continue my explanation for my uninvited arrival.

Carole grabbed my arm as if to stop me before I could say anything else.

"Angela! She said bluntly. 'We know about the book. Tony has read it, he has a copy. Please come in and have a cuppa. He will be so pleased to see you".

As she lead me through the door, she explained he was upstairs on his Kidney Dialysis machine and that he would be down in a few minutes. I had heard about the trials of his ill health, over the years but wasn't aware just how serious things had got.

I sat down, staring at the staircase waiting for Tony to reveal himself. I hadn't seen him for nearly forty years but the strange thing was It all felt so 'natural' to be sitting there, as it was all a 'planned' part of a bigger picture.

I heard movement, as the sight of his feet appeared at the top of the staircase. The rest of him was revealed with each step he took. He had the same trim shape and the same timeless dress sense too, with blue jeans , a Jimi Hendrix T –shirt and a pair of round blue tinted glasses like his brothers,. Nothing changed there, I thought. He must have been in earshot to who the caller was at his door.

As he appeared with a welcoming smile and said instantly…..

'Awww Great to see you Ange….. And look at me' he said, giving apology… pointing to his shoulder length hair, as he explained …. 'I only had it cut this short, last week, for the very first time'

He knew he would have been remembered by me and many others back in the day, for his ' Osbourne' 'trade mark', the flowing long locks.

Him and 'Ozzy' looked like twins and still did, apart from Tony having the shorter styled hair now.

Whilst we sat having tea and reminiscing, I had felt a great presence of 'spirit' around him as he mentioned the roller coaster of a journey, his troubled life had took, battling tragedy and illness.

He said 'There is something I must tell you, you know when I received that letter from you, I think there was a 'dual' reason and purpose to it. As you had written and concluded your visions which seem to coincide, queite rightly, with 'our John's'(Ozzy's) infamous quad bike crash.

There was something else that happened that week, it seemed as if all 'Hell' broke loose in our family. It wasn't just 'our John and his quad bike crash…. 'You see Ange, that week I lost my son Danny. He died. Your letter was so, so timely. It bought me comfort in a way that I can't explain.

I just want to say Thankyou and I'm so proud of you, proud to of known you'.

I felt a healing process happening, as we 'let out' and shared, some of our darkest times, but never the less our humour picked us up in interval moments, as I made him smile through his tearful blue eyes.

I was consciously aware I was sitting with a 'bag full' of emotions and an immense feeling of spiritual presence, which confirmed, what I'd initially felt.

I felt I had to change the subject before it got too 'heavy' as you could see he was struggling and wanting to keep things up beat.

'How's your John' I asked, changing the subject.

'Oh he's okay, he's great, he keeps in touch regularly. I was telling him all about you and your book.' He added.

I jumped in eagerly and asked..

Oh, yeah, what did he say?'.

'He said 'She's 'bleeping' scary she is!' or words to that effect.

I could just visualise it.

I quick wittedly replied. 'Yes I can just 'see' the headlines now, 'Medium scares 'the Prince of Darkness' hey! Tone'

We both laughed, if we hadn't, we would of cried.

When I left that day, I just knew it was going to be the last time I'd sit and chat with him in this psychical life, at least.

It was recently but several years later, I received a text from his relatives, informing me that Tony had passed away a couple of days beforehand and that he had spoke of me in his last hours.

Those words impacted on my soul but I knew he was truly happy now, as I and he, had no doubt that he'd be reunited with his Parents, his wife and his beloved son Danny.

And as for my 'Black Sabbath' roadie Neil, he reappeared for another 'timed' and scheduled sitting.

As we sat down to commence. There was someone named Ronnie who I'd felt, had not long passed to spirit.

I began ~

'Ronnie was a character, and I could see a collection of Garden Gnomes, he had collected, it was one of his simple pleasures in life'. I said.

The statement made Neil smile, as he knew then, exactly who I was 'receiving' from but again Neil didn't confirm who it was till I had finished relaying what Ronnie had to say. I continued…..

'He speaks of a large painting of himself. He would often joke about it. Neil caught onto what Ronnie meant and laughed aloud. Ronnie then gave me a feeling of a great sense of seriousness and guilt as he so wanted to send love to his Son and apologise to him for not being there for him in this life.

Neil had grasped everything to what Ronnie had communicated.

It was obvious to me that Ronnie was linked to Neil's work and it was someone he'd had a good bond with too and still did, by the sounds of it.

Ronnie repeated himself over and over again about the message to his son. It was obvious he wanted Neil to pass on this message as it seemed of paramount importance, as I could hear and feel the urgency in his voice.

'Well' I said, looking towards Neil for confirmation.
.
'I'm shaking here' he said 'The only Ronnie I know that I have links with, is Ronnie James Dio, a member of Black Sabbath.. You must know that? He said looking at me with eyebrows raised.

'I was never a fan' I exclaimed, 'besides I was more into Tony, Ozzys brother.

He began explaining. 'I never expected anything like this…especially from Ronnie. Ronnie only died a few weeks ago. I missed his funeral as I was touring at the time, but I am going to the States soon and I do plan to make a visit to his family to pay my respects.

He continued.

'You know, I had worked with him for years and I never knew he had a Son. I only found out recently because I heard he had attended his funeral, that surprised me, as I never heard Ronnie mention him but I will pass on that message it's the least I can do for him. And your right about the Garden Gnomes', he laughed as he continued to say.

'He did have a collection of them. It didn't say too much about his rock'n'roll image though and as for the painting, It wasn't exactly an oil painting as such, Its discovery, was when we was flying over an Eastern-block country and there was this great big Muriel of Ronnie's face painted on the side of a block of Flats, the 'sight' of which became the butt of long standing joke.'Mmm… by the sounds of it, he seems okay', he said finally.

Neil now had to run his last 'errand' for his Band Member and become once again the Roadie but this time with a 'message' to tell.

.
.

.
.

Clare's Shamrock

My friends Clare and Joan are identical twins whom I first met when I was seven years old. They lived close by in the small village in which we lived. We attended the same Catholic primary and secondary school. Most of our waking hours were spent together. At school we were often mistaken for sisters because of our very dark hair and fair complexions. We were quite happy to live up to the idea. I was the only one at school who could tell them apart, and I was often asked, by teachers and pupils alike, which one was which. I would revel in the fun of confusing people by telling them the wrong name at times. Little did I know the friendship I made then would last a lifetime. Even though we grew up and went our separate ways, we still found time to meet up on occasion, catching up on what life had 'dished out' to us.

A bond was always there. Coincidently, each one of us had ended up being single mothers. And it was during those times I began to play a significant part in both of their destinies.

It was a few days before my birthday when I felt compelled to invite Joan out for the evening, as I had recently found out she was on her own once again. I invited her to join myself and a few friends, as I planned to go into Birmingham City to see a live band to celebrate. A visit to the city was becoming a rare thing for me, but I made an exception as my gut feeling had told me I had to go, and prior to the event the name of the band kept cropping up in unusual places. For me that was a sign. That evening turned out to be fateful for Joan.

During the evening, a man walked directly up to me and asked me to dance. Usually I would have obliged, but when I opened my mouth I found myself saying, 'Oh no, thank you, but please dance with my friend, you and her would make a lovely couple.'

Little did any of us realize at the time, but I had just introduced Joan to her future husband. That fateful evening was 15 years ago, and they are still together to this day, happily married and living in Ireland with their new-found families. I often visit them. I look back and think how my instinctive gut feelings had played a part in shaping Joan's happier future. It was all meant to be.

The part I played in Clare's life was something entirely different. Something that I had premonitions about in nothing like the same way. What unfolded on her pathway was totally different, but mapped out by God all the same.

A few years ago I was told by Joan that Clare's marriage had broken down and she and her children were moving to a house near to me. Bringing our pathways close together once more. Thereafter we would often meet up. Sharing our daily loads with each other was so easy, even though years had passed in our lives up till then, keeping us apart. The way we spoke to each other, it was as if time hadn't lapsed. We were like schoolgirls together again, but this time with women's worldly knowledge. She seemed very together and positive, but would often seek words of comfort and encouragement from me. I would give these to her, happily, but I never seemed to be inspired to tell her anything really profound. She knew about me match-making for her sister, but she did not know or understand the full extent of my 'gift'.

Something that I 'sensed' about Clare unfolded in a phone call from Joan late one night. She had called to tell me that Clare had been diagnosed with leukaemia and that she planned to move in with Clare and stay with her for as long as it took her to recover. Joan and their older sister Doreen planned to care for Clare. Clare was starting her chemotherapy almost immediately.

It was a terrible shock. The recent thoughts I'd had, had been confirmed, as I remembered a meeting with Clare a week or so before. Clare had been complaining about a chest infection that seemed to have lingered for weeks, and she was just going to the doctor's for some blood tests. I 'sensed' then that something was dreadfully wrong, but dismissed the idea and kept quiet about my thoughts.

In the months that followed, I continued to visit Clare at home and in hospital. Clare was remarkable. She just seemed to get on with it. I knew she must have had her very own private emotional moments. She seemed very together all the same. I tried to keep her mind occupied on other things as we would talk about everything and anything but her illness, unless she mentioned it. We still laughed and joked, even when she was prescribed a hairpiece in preparation for when she lost her beautiful head of hair. Great care and attention had gone into the style and colour to match her hair. She was now blonde. She had gone grey at a very early age and no longer had the dark hair we three were renowned for. The hairpiece had just been given to her as I arrived on a visit to her, one day in hospital. Clare was eager to see what I looked like blonde. She egged me on to try on the hairpiece. As I did, a nurse popped her head round the door of the room. The nurse looked confused and gave me a scornful look and tutted. We giggled like two schoolgirls up to mischief.

It was a case of if we didn't laugh we would have cried. For my part, I felt helpless. I would always ask her, as I left, whether there was anything she really fancied to eat. I always promised to bring her goodies on my next visit. I never arrived empty-handed. Whatever food I brought her, it would always include two chocolate cream éclairs, her favourite. Mind, it was more about me needing to help sustain someone whose weight was dwindling before my eyes. It was a natural reaction, but I felt it was the very least I could do.

When Clare was due home after her treatment, I decided to call an old schoolfriend of ours, Maggie. Maggie had been the local doctor's daughter. She had also been something of the school 'agony aunt', as people would often turn to her for advice. She had healing qualities about her even back then, so it didn't surprise me that she turned out to be an alternative therapist. Maggie and I planned to visit Clare and Joan at home, thereby bonding our friendship once again, as we had been quite a foursome at school.

As all four of us sat round Clare's kitchen table reminiscing about school and the antics we'd got up to, we laughed heartedly. We talked about a vast number of subjects, but there was one subject I never brought up in front of Clare while she was ill: my work as a medium. I felt the subject was too close to death.

We'd all sat listening attentively to Clare, rambling on about her memories of her childhood, about the many visits she had made to Ireland and how much she loved the place, and in recent years the amount of times she had brought shamrock seeds back home with her. And how she'd tried to plant it in various places, in the hope that she could grow her own here, .in England, but that she'd eventually given up on the idea. She said she had come to the conclusion that shamrock will only grow on Irish soil. I agreed with her entirely, as I had tried the same thing time and time again. We went on to talk about what we were going to do when she got better, as Clare lived in hope of a bone marrow transplant.

Then, almost randomly in the conversation, she turned to me and said she had gone to see a medium some years ago. She told me that the medium had told her that her father was in Spirit and that her father knew that she often sat and spoke to his photograph. It was the first time she had mentioned the subject since she had been ill. I told Clare the woman sounded like a good medium and that I was in no doubt that her father would be listening to Clare's every word. Clare's eyes filled with tears. The tears rolled down her small thin, pale face. It was the first time in the months of her illness she had let her emotions escape in front of her friends. We sat in silence for a while as tears filled all our eyes and fell. We didn't say one word. We didn't have to. The realization of all her pain hit us all. Then in unison we must have thought the same thing: how ridiculous we looked. It was almost in embarrassment that we all began to titter and then laugh hysterically at the sight of us all crying. Maggie then said, with perfect timing, 'It's time for some more tea, I think.' She always had that knack of knowing what to say.

In the days that followed, Clare was admitted back to hospital. It was then that Joan told me that she was terminal. Everything that I had 'sensed' but had denied and kept to myself was becoming a reality.

Clare's family, out of pure love, decided not to tell her as they feared her spirit would give up the fight and leave. Understandably they wanted to keep her as long as they could.

Clare's life was prolonged by the fact she was an identical twin and that Joan, unquestioningly, donated some of her own white blood cells to help strengthen Clare's immune system, though sadly for a short time only.

It was during this time, on my hospital visits, that I would see Clare's father's spirit standing beside her bed, stroking her head. I never mentioned it until I heard him say in my mind, 'It's OK, ask her about me.'

I asked, without any apprehension whatsoever, 'Clare ... Have you ever dreamt about your father while you've been poorly?' I said.

Joan, who was sitting beside me, she just looked at me in surprise. She probably wondered where the question was leading to.

'Funny you should say that, this time in hospital I've done nothing *but* dream about him every single night,' Clare replied.

'Aah, Clare ...' I said. 'How lovely, that's his way of letting you know he is watching over you, love.' She smiled a comforted smile. She never questioned me.

In reality I knew that he was waiting to help her cross over to the Other Side.

Joan looked at me pensively, deep in thought. I delivered the message in its entirety to Joan as we walked along the hospital corridors towards the canteen. Joan was never a true believer, very much a sceptic then, like a lot of people. I told her again what I saw of her father's spirit. She told me she would very much like to believe that. I told her she just had to. Her father would really want her to know that. Over coffee, a thought came in from Joan's father's spirit once again. This time it was about his own passing.

'Joan, your father passed twice, didn't he?' I asked.

'What do you mean?' she asked, intrigued.

'I sense he passed away and was resuscitated, stayed a few days longer and then finally passed away,' I said.

'That's right, but how do you know that? You weren't around when he died.' I could feel her mind ticking over everything I had said. 'I do so want to believe,' she said.

I felt it was only a matter of time. Perhaps when she was given her own spiritual comforts, or maybe now that my seeds of thought had now been planted, they would take root and would bloom in time.

Clare was later able to spend some time back at home. She looked very aged and frail. She had to have large doses of oxygen to help her move around.

It was my birthday once again. I arrived at Clare's house with Maggie, saying that we had come to take Clare to dinner. I had told Maggie that I sensed Clare would not be with us much longer and that I had planned to go away the following weekend for a short break, so wanted to see her while I had the chance.

Clare was delighted to be going out. Her mind was eager but her body was weak. She had difficulty moving around and looked almost skeletal. Nevertheless, nothing seemed to deter her. Joan and I literally carried her down the steps of house and awkwardly steered her into my car. This raised a warm smile or two.

We arrived at the restaurant arm in arm, all linked together. We swept Clare across the restaurant floor to our table, her feet barely touching the floor. Clare's plate was stacked high. She amazed us all by devouring the lot.

We smiled and giggled above the underlying sadness; seated round a table we ate what was to become our final meal with all four of us together.

That day happened to be the last time I would see Clare alive. She passed away a few days later, that weekend while I was away.

I believe when she 'crossed over' it was a bright, beautiful sunny day, and she was surrounded by her children and other loved ones. She was given the grace of time to say all she wanted to say, and in those final moments Clare's father's spirit collected her. His presence was confirmed and felt by her older sister Doreen. God had granted Clare the perfect passing.

I received the news as I arrived home. I was obviously very upset, but I knew it was not the last I would hear from my friend Clare. I eventually fell asleep that evening and woke up the next morning realizing that Clare had tried her best to communicate to me during the night in my dreams. I understood my emotions were overriding my full senses, naturally causing barriers. I spoke to Joan the next day. My intention was to tell her what I had 'received'. To my surprise, when I did, Joan had the full explanation of my dream.

I'd told Joan, 'I could see Clare standing in the distance looking lovely and so smartly dressed. She was back to her usual self. She was waving at me, but the unusual thing was I couldn't hear her. The even stranger thing was she stood with a large suitcase at her feet. And she also showed me a piece of paper with numbers on it. I tried to fathom it out, Joan, but I woke up puzzled and upset … Also in the dream I spoke to Clare, saying, "No, Clare … You don't take a suitcase to the Spirit World … besides that, I hope you are trying to give me the lottery numbers, eh, love?"… trying to cheer myself up with the thought. I obviously knew they meant something else. But the initial thought made me smile, though.'

As I said this, it was if a light went on in Joan's mind – or maybe the seeds I had planted had begun to take root. 'I know what that's all about,' Joan said. 'Clare must know about the plans we have just made. We've decided that the weekend after the funeral all the family is coming over to Ireland to stay with me for the week.'

I interrupted. 'Clare's obviously got her suitcase packed, then! She'll probably arrive before you get there.'

'Well, I hope she's got the kettle on, ready,' Joan replied. Joan continued to explain, 'I know what the numbers on the piece of paper mean, too. It must be that she is trying to tell us that she knows that we have found the piece of paper with her bank account numbers on. The one she told us about just before she passed.' It seemed Joan's awareness was growing. It all made perfect sense to Joan, and that's what really mattered.

I hoped that Joan's newfound knowledge of Spirit World communication was enabling her to speak with such ease, and that it was giving her comfort knowing that Clare hadn't really gone. Sometimes the wisdom of the Spirit World cannot always be given, as such, but only gained through one's own experiences.

During that week, I gave a demonstration in a hotel in Worcester. There I met a woman who gave me a message. Almost apologetically, she said that she could sense a young woman around me who had recently passed. I told her it was my friend and that she was not buried as yet. That seemed to surprise this woman. She went on to say that there was something about an angel on a stone … for the life of me I couldn't think of anything in relation to that. The woman suggested that maybe my friend wanted an angel on her gravestone … I dismissed the thought, though, as it definitely wasn't Clare's taste in things.

When I arrived home, the penny dropped. It wasn't an 'angel on a stone'. It was an angel *in* a stone. I remembered that when Clare was first admitted to hospital I took her a little gift of a small glass stone with a model of an angel inside. She'd asked what it was it for. I'd told her she just had to hold it in her hand and ask her angels to watch over her. She'd welcomed it; I wasn't too sure whether she would use it, but it was nice to think that she was asking about it now. I told Joan about the 'angel in a stone'. She promised she would search for it among Clare's belongings.

The day before the funeral, Joan, Maggie and I went to visit Clare at the funeral parlour to say our last goodbyes and to ensure she looked her best for her big day. Joan placed a few treasured photographs and mementos with her. She then surprised me by presenting me with the angel in a stone and asking me to place it with Clare. As I did, Joan piped up, 'You should really be placing two chocolate cream éclairs with that.' I agreed with her.

Then Joan and I made Clare look pretty. Joan styled her short cropped hair and I painted her nails, ensuring she looked the way she would want to look, as she was a bit of a perfectionist when it came to her make-up and nails.

The evening after the funeral Joan suggested that the three of us should go out for a meal before Joan's return to Ireland. Joan thought it uncanny that I suggested we go to Sophia's, an Italian restaurant that was relatively new. Apparently it had been one of Clare's favourite places.

When we arrived and were shown to our seats, we all became conscious of the single empty chair that stood at our table. Joan and Maggie looked at the chair, then glanced at me as if for reassurance. 'Don't worry, Clare's here with us,' I said. 'She wouldn't miss this place for the world.'

We all smiled at the thought, but sitting there around a table with an empty chair was a sad sight all the same.

A week or so later, I was due to deliver services at the Psychic Truth Society in Liverpool. As I arrived I was met by the warden, a lovely lady named Connie, who said that she had got my rooms all prepared for me. She made a point of saying that she had put a few extra nice things in the fridge, also. I wasn't surprised at all by what I found there. Connie must have been inspired by Clare's spirit, as there in the fridge were two chocolate cream éclairs. This was no coincidence. There is no such thing. I made this part of my address that evening ...

Almost a year to the day of the anniversary of Clare's passing, a real moment of 'faith' was created in which the influence of Clare's spirit played a part. It was then that my daughter, who was heavily pregnant with her second child, moved into Clare's old house.

The day she moved in, I was giving her a helping hand. While waiting for the removal van to arrive, I suggested we tidy up the front garden, as the house had stood empty for a while and the weeds had had time to spread. With my trowel in hand, I bent down to clear the weeds, which I could see had grown in between the flagstones surrounding the front doorstep. I almost squealed with emotion and delight at what I discovered. It wasn't weeds that were growing around Clare's doorstep. It was shamrock. It was 'Clare's shamrock'. My daughter was puzzled for a moment. She wondered why I was holding a 'weed' in my hand with tears in my eyes, shouting, 'Look! Look! It's Clare ...'

I went on to explain about our conversation about shamrock. I'm so thankful that my daughter understands my strange and wonderful life. We were both touched by what we found. We were witnessing something very special flourishing before our eyes.

My next thought was to phone Joan and tell her. I knew she would want to see it for herself, so I gathered a few strands and pressed them and made them into bookmarks. I posted them, with a note saying 'Clare's Shamrock' to Joan a day or so later.

The shamrock has continued to grow. We have left it to wander free, just like Clare's spirit. We have allowed it to become a beautiful reminder of true faith to us all.

It is humbling, knowing that Clare's loved ones now know that Clare is still able to communicate in profound and subtle ways. And that she will always continue to do so, whenever and wherever she chooses.

There have been many times when I have 'sensed' Clare's presence, but never more so than when I visit Ireland. This is where she often 'walks' alongside her twin sister Joan and me. Just as she used to. Letting us know that all is well.

A SOLDIERS TALE

Approximately 18 months ago, when I was coming to the end of a service in a Spiritualist church in Telford, I saw the spirit of a young soldier standing behind a middle-aged couple in the front row. I could tell by his uniform he had passed in a more recent conflict. I asked the couple if I could speak to them, as I had a soldier waiting to communicate with them. I noticed the man move about in his chair a little uncomfortably, as if he were preparing himself in some way to receive his message, as I told him, 'I have a soldier named Jimmy with me, who passed away in conflict and he is mentioning something about Northampton.'

The man coughed and cleared his throat nervously as he said, 'That is my friend and comrade. We were together when he got killed in the Falklands. He was from Northampton.'

I could see tears fill his eyes as he spoke. The lady next to him gripped his hand.

'Jimmy would have had stripes on his arm and he is showing me a signet ring. I believe he was due to get married. Is that not so?'

'Yes,' the man replied, his colour seeming to change. I was feeling totally absorbed by Jimmy's spirit as I continued, 'Jimmy says you are still in touch with his family. I believe you have received some news from them this week?' I could hear Jimmy talking loud and clear. It was a very powerful communication.

'Yes,' said the man, 'I have received a letter from his parents informing me that his sister has passed over recently.'

'You know they are together now, don't you? Jimmy tells me he came to greet her and to cross her over. Jimmy desperately wants to get a message through to his parents but he tells me that they don't believe in the afterlife,' I said.

'No, that's true, they don't,' he confirmed.

'But you must tell them that he is OK and that he says he is aware that his parents are going to a big parade soon. And he knows his mother is determined to get there. No matter what, and that you're going, too?' I said.

'That's right. Next year is the 25th anniversary of the Falklands Conflict and there is a big parade in London to commemorate it. His parents are planning to go and his mother is so determined regardless of the fact that she is in a wheelchair.'

'Jimmy wants you to know that he will be marching alongside you all.' Jimmy's spirit had taken over and touched everyone in the congregation. There wasn't a dry eye in the house.

But just before he left me I found not only my thoughts but also my actions were taking part in a finale totally instrumented by Jimmy's spirit. I said, 'Before he goes he doesn't want to salute you like this,' as I gave a demonstration of a regular Army salute. I then found myself doing a little comical salute, twisting my fingers round in the centre of my forehead as I said, 'He wants to salute you like this.'

'He would have been court-marshalled if he was ever caught doing a salute like that!' his comrade said. 'But that was the last thing he did, before he was killed,' he said, as he smiled through his tears. Jimmy's finale broke the silence from the congregation as they gasped and applauded.

It seemed Jimmy's presence was with me for the rest of the evening, as he still felt close by as I drove home. I thought it would be interesting to find out more about the Northampton Falklands hero, as there were only 256 British soldiers killed in the Falklands and I didn't think it would be too difficult to find out one who'd come from the Northampton area and was named Jimmy. I will never forget Jimmy and the power of his communication. I often tell his story.

On one occasion I'd just finished talking about him when a friend of mine, who liked an occasional flutter on the horses, asked me if I could give her a tip for the day. I gave in to her persuasion and as she handed me the newspaper a name caught my eye. The horse was called 'A Soldier's Tale'. It seemed to have Jimmy's name written all over it and it was a good price, too: 14 to 1. My friend seemed rather surprised when she realized the coincidence. I told her to have faith. She was even more surprised when it won! I was as thrilled as she was, even though I didn't have a bet on it. It just confirmed my belief that Spirit confirms its existence with strange coincidences to give people true faith, which is a belief in the unseen.

Another strange coincidence unfolded the very next day when I was reading the Sunday papers. The sporting headlines read, 'A Soldier's Tale: A Real Hero'. There was a write-up about the horse. Its jockey made an emotional tribute, saying that A Soldier's Tale was the horse that 'came back from the dead', as it had been near to the point of being put down twice. But he was a fighter, so tough and so brave despite his many fractures, colic, surgery and pieces of stomach having been removed. A real hero, that's what they called him. I have no doubt that Jimmy's spirit influenced my choice of horse. It was such a fitting horse for Jimmy's memory. I wouldn't be surprised if Jimmy's spirit was on the back of that horse!

I chose to put his story in this book to help him filter his message through to his beloved family, for he gave
the greatest love in laying down his life for his friends, his comrades and his country.

Bless you, Jimmy.

Marian

Access to the "spirit' of 'Our lady', the Virgin Mary, almost seemed like a 'birth right', as culturally and religiously speaking, being born into the Catholic faith opened a door to her, as she played a part in fermenting my 'spiritual' foundations, helping to create the 'Sense' of 'Spiritualty' that I hold today.

I first recognised her name, as it was part of my Grandmother Kathleen Murphy's daily vocabulary.

Mary being undoubtedly the world's most famous woman, the only woman revered so highly, who'd lived a mortal life and went on to become the 'Queen of all Angels' in Gods Kingdom. Mary is a name that was and is mentioned in Catholic households on a daily basis alongside Jesus, of course and all the other Angels and saints too.

Mentioned both in prayer and in lingual expressions, as we Catholics would call upon her help and her intercession in moments of despair, stress and want. Mary is an example of Motherhood and Miracles. It is through her intercession to Jesus, we would ask 'favours', constantly.

It is without doubt that the Spirit of 'Our Lady' had left a carved impression in my 'psyche' from a very early start in life, both religiously and culturally but most all her 'place' in the context of true 'spirituality'.

I can't say I've ever had an exquisite 'Marian' experience as such, as I have, on more that one occasion, been asked by Clergy. In response I would tell them of my experiences and how I, at different stages of my life, and at very poignant times, particularly within moments of deep despair, those moments when Mary had left an 'impression', an imprint in my questionable mind and soul. It was through the power of Prayer, her spirit, her intercession, left a larger than life impression in varying degrees with me.

So I can honestly say her 'style' of 'communication' has held a special, a revered, place in my heart and understandably the hearts of my Spirit Guides.

My first encounter of her, was very questionable but never less remained in a haze of thoughts, which I have held and tried to decipher all my life, I debated it, whether it was dream or my imagination but my reaction to the small' 'impression' at the time was one of a strange feeling of 'upliftment' even if only, for a short while but it's memory left a place open, where in future I could go and feel safe and sit in the solace it gave.

It happened during a traumatic time as a small child, being separated from my mother, whilst living in Convent care, the darkest and most isolating place.

I was approximately four years old. I remember every lengthy second of my time in the Convent.

It was shortly after, one of my infamous temper tantrum episodes, where I had been isolated, locked up in a room, until my silence had returned or the nuns want of my mode of 'surrender and helplessness' to break me, but it was a case of me getting to a realisation, that no one would really listen or deal with my plea's.

They just couldn't cope with the lengthy screams and shouts that went on for hours. They had no idea how to console a child, as forced control was their only method, which didn't seem to work in my case.

In hindsight I had no doubt, my soul was being prayed for at the time.

I would be placed in isolation regularly as a pattern emerged, particularly after being wrenched away from my mother. It was when time was being called, after her hourly allowance of a weekly visit, came to a harrowing end with my 'endless' screams.

To avoid this reaction happening, the Mother Superior ordered that my mother's visits to me, alone, to stop altogether. But her visits to my elder brothers and sisters would continue to take place. It seemed so devastatingly unfair.

It seemed I lived oblivious to all the other children in the Convent as I spent most of my time like others, being 'withdrawn' and playing in the imagination of our 'own' little minds and worlds. Our souls were wrapped up in layers of fear.

I like everyone else constantly lived in fear of being told off by not 'doing' the right thing or for not having the adequacy to follow strict instructions to a totally new and alien regime.

There were many fearful moments that struck throughout the day, one was the nightly procedure in the prevention of bed-wetting, and that idea was attached to a bell, which rang in the night to wake you up, to remind you to make use of the potty under your bed. For most of the children in the Dormitory, the bell and the Potty were never 'in sync'.

The Nuns 'failed' to understand that 'fear' was the cause, of bed wetting, not laziness, for which punishment was the result of the latter.

When supper arrived each night, we were given hot milk and a piece of toast. I soon learned that it was a 'sin' to waste food as Nuns would order you to eat every morsel. And if you blurted out, that you didn't like any one particular thing on your plate, the plate was removed and you went hungry. So often I would be hungry at night. I'd eat my toast though, but not the crust, which I didn't like. Leaving the crust became a fearful ordeal. I would panick as I'd shove the crust up my sleeve, an make plans to seek disposel of them later in various places that gave into opportunity, one such down place was in-between, my brother's bedsheets. To my horror the crust was discovered by a Nun first, I remember crying with him, as he was being punished. Both of us too scared, to give any explanation.

I was often scolded and told by one particular Nun, who I'd unsettled, during the course of my many tantrums.

I remember her cutting 'word's as she shrieked at me.

'You may not be seeing your mother again, so you're best to get used to it'!! .

Her cruel words attempted to 'shock' me into quietness and chip at my soul. But my soul deep down knew that wasn't the case.

The temper tantrum episodes remained spasmodic. I couldn't keep them under control. They were a part of me, an explosive expression of emotions, triggered by thoughts and experiences, which I couldn't fully understand.

I remember being collected from isolation by a Nun after one such episode had finally subsided.

I was taken to join the other children as they filed out into the spacious grounds of the Convent towards another part of the buildings. Our path took us past a life size statue of Mary, which was set in a rock, were a small type Grotto had been created. We all had to stop and gather in order of line, as we were instructed and shown, how to stand, placing our hands together with fingers pointing upwards, with our heads bowed in reverence, as the Nun recited a prayer in a language I didn't understand. I remember feeling a heightened fearful state of awareness. Not wanting to do anything out of place or order, or anything which would be deemed as wrong or sinful.

It was a moment amongst the confusion, during the Nuns orders. I felt like I'd gone into a trance- like state, totally withdrawn, as I took a glimpse of the Statues beautiful face.

I seemed fixated upon it, and that of me. I was oblivious to my surroundings, it was then in my tiny child like mind I was convinced the 'lady' statue smiled at me, as when she did, it seem to induce, a lovely warm, peaceful calm, feeling that seem to pass through out my body, from my head to my feet.

.It seemed to stay with me for a few seconds but it left me feeling content, if only for a while.

This was the only questionable, possibly imaginative but comforting 'memory' of that traumatic period. It was only the smile that was 'questionable' but the feelings seemed 'real.' that followed.

In fact the true understanding and explanation of such feelings which I discovered later in life, that I have been a witness to, time and time again with myself and many other Christian people and seekers such like. These feelings in such environments and want, especially during prayer state, are often described, when a 'healing' has taken place. In Christian terms it is described and regarded as the receiving of the 'Gift of the Holy Spirit'.

When I first confessed this experience to a Priest I was told simply, to accept it as 'Blessing.'

So my first infant impressionable encounter of Mary and the Holy Spirit would not be the last so it seemed.

For over the decades at poignant times, Mary 'Our Lady', her intercession would leave an 'impression' on some of the soul-searching, devastating experiences and circumstances that I would find myself in.

My 'Marian' style encounters continued not only for my sake but for the sake of others too.

It was during the early days of son's ill health I was searching for answers, not only to the many aspects of my daily life. I was looking for spiritual answers to 'why and for what purpose' had life, handed me, yet another 'dark' period. Some people lose faith during such times but in fact it drew me closer to God. I was praying each quiete moment I had, particularly late at night when I found it hard to sleep.

To help me sleep I remembered one person's piece of advice which, was to read a book, as 'it will take your mind off things and make you sleepy.'

It was during that almost sleepless days, I came across a second- hand book shop on my travels, whilst seeing to other people's problems and spiritual needs.

I meandered in and within minutes found a book that seemed to be 'waiting' for me.

It was a theological book called 'Miracles of Mary' - Apparitions, legends and, the miraculous works of the

Blessed Virgin Mary written and compiled by Michael S .Durham

A subject that fascinated me, little did I know it would 'impress me' in more ways one. It was a book compiled of more than sixty stories of where 'Mary' had 'appeared 'to saints and sinners alike, leaving 'messages' and 'signs' of hope and even miracles behind.

It was at the end of yet another very stressful day. I lay in bed and started to read it. My concentration was 'shot' so I just skipped though the book looking at the beautiful pictures of famous paintings and statues of Mary. I was surprised, when I read that she had 'appeared' most recently in Chicago and New York these two such places, relating to Marian experiences I'd never heard of, amidst my upbringing or Catholic circle of friends.

I'd only heard of Knock in Ireland and of course the most adored, The 'Miracles' at 'Lourdes' in the south of France.

After I scanned through almost all, the pictures, I came across a prayer, dedicated to Mary the Blessed Virgin. I read it and then fell asleep, exhausted.

Surprisingly, I woke the next morning feeling very refreshed after such a heavy, well needed sleep.

It wasn't till my young daughter came down for breakfast and spoke so eagerly, of her experience she'd had, during the night, that I started to question and connect her experience to more than just a coincidence.

'Oh mom' she said. I've had such a 'strange' dream. I have never, ever dreamt of a holy person before, but it was like this…. 'In the dream you and I were sleeping in my bed, in the loft room upstairs and we lay there asleep, then we both woke up and saw 'Mary' 'Our lady' standing at the foot of the bed. She looked beautiful, she was surrounded by a big ball of light, that filled the room and then this lovely warm, feeling went through my body and then I woke from the dream thinking and questioning, 'was that real?' Did that really happen?

"What do you make of that mom",. She asked.

I gave my daughter an honest and comforting but simple reply, as I had always encouraged my children to talk of their dreams, as often there is a hidden 'spiritual message or more often a 'message' from a loved one in heaven.

A memory echoed in my head, as I told her, in a special way, it was a very good dream to have and to take it, as a Blessing.

I later, examined the 'experience' even more. I concluded that I'd had a blessing too.

In summary, it was a response, an 'impression' and with perfect timing, that on the same night, after reading a 'dedicated' book and sending up a 'want' in a prayer, an 'answer, a response' came in the form of a 'blessing.' It would have made no sense to me, if Mary had appeared in my dream, as I would have dismissed it by thinking that the pictures of book, had left an impression on my mind. But Mary chose to go to my innocent daughter's dream, as she slept in the room above me. My daughter was made a 'witness', to the receiving of that 'lovely warm feeling' she described, as what we already know, as the 'Holy Spirit'.

The subject of the dream came up in conversation years later during a church group meeting. I explained it to a Priest I knew well, and one that was aware of my humour.

It was told in all seriousness and in awe of its beauty. Again the priest echoed the explanation as he couldn't doubt it and told me to accept the experience as a blessing. I quipped up this time with a wry smile at him and said

"So I don't have to make my loft into a shrine then Father?' He smiled back with a 'knowing' 'glint' in his eye.

It was years later on one of my adventurous times visiting Ireland. I had the idea to do a fly- drive holiday with my youngest daughter in tow ,and my best friend whose name happens to be Mary too (nee-Quigley) and her granddaughter, who was of similar age to my daughter. We were a jolly foursome planning to discover as much of the coast lines of Ireland as we could in the ten days allocated, calling in on friends and family along the way.

We didn't plan to visit the Marian Shrine at Knock but after loosing our way along the roads .We noticed we had almost arrived at the destination unexpectedly, as we were about to give rest from driving. Our arrival had been 'mapped' it wasn't a case of a series of 'wrong' turns after all. I had special intention to have a Mass said for my ailing son, as he was and is always in the forefront of my prayers.

We were amazed at the number of souvenir shops in such a tiny Village. The girls soon got laden with souvenirs and trinkets of a holy nature, as they began to shop.

We diligently queued up within a parade of people who wanted to touch the stones on which 'Our lady Mary the Blessed Virgin had once been seen standing on, in the Apparition, which was witnessed by a number of people nearly a hundred years before.

The large stones had been imbedded in a wall, which was now, part of the church dedicated to Mary. There was also a natural stream of water which is believed to hold healing properties. This had been piped around the grounds to a number of free flowing water taps.

So the done thing, it seemed, was to touch the stones, go into the church, place your prayer petition and then Bless yourself with the holy water.

The limitless holy water was available to you and as much as you wanted to gather. Plastic bottles of various shapes and sizes, was available to fill at your leisure.

I was amazed at the commercialisation of its surroundings but I rationalised it and put it all in to an understandable perspective.

I began to concentrate on the story of the Miracle and miracles attached to the Shrine as I witnessed and 'sensed' the immense feeling of love and adoration amidst the people, that had travelled near and far to visit this 'sacred ground'.

My turn came to touch the stones, I ran my hands over their craggy texture. I was taken by surprise with one of them. I was convinced I could feel 'heat,.' as I shouted back at my friend.

"Mary' I can feel heat, there's heat coming from this stone. I can feel the heat! I said repeatedly, convincing myself something supernatural was happening.

There was an Irish lady in the queue behind me who must of overheard, as she repeated what I said.

"Jeeez….Mother of God… she can feel the heat!" She said, almost rejoicing.

Her voice and statement caused a ripple of excitement in the queue but never the less they all seemed very 'receptive' to what I'd said, as they blessed themselves with the sign of the cross.

With a twinkle in her eye, the old lady added

"That's it! Our lady must want to say something to you, now you go in there and say your prayers", she instructed, pointing through the window of the beautiful glass fronted church, which displayed the white marble statues, depicting, the Holy Apparition.

I did just that. I did what I was told.

I put in my prayer petition and I was sure 'Our lady' heard every word.

Before we left the Shrine. I took the opportunity to stock up on my Crucifixes, Rosary beads and a couple of half gallon bottles of holy water, tools, for my work back home, involving all types of Blessings, and Soul Rescues.

It wasn't long before the holy water was in action, in fact moments, as it leaked all over my little girls feet, in the car whilst travelling, her little socks where soaked.

I smiled as I told her, 'take it as a blessing'.

In hindsight, someone must of 'heard' me., (for it was a couple years later, her tom boy nature, got the better of her., She took up playing football and her talented blessed feet, got her noticed by Aston Villa Girls Football Club and she became an integral part of the team, for a few years, during which they won a couple of major cups.)

My Footballing son, caught on to this 'questionable' coincidence and prior to each of his games, he began 'blessing' his boots with the holy water that remained, and needless to say he has had success in a footballing career.

'Belief' is all it takes. Anything is possible with a Faith

But Mary always holds a special place in my heart, along my spiritual journey. For Mary's works of communication and miracles continue in profound and subtle ways. Her help like all those loved ones in heaven, those mere mortals who are sent with a message is 'received' with love and honour as we know it stems from the love of God.

I've learned to treat each day as if it were a 'miracle, because it simply is. And each day miracles do happen. The fact that I do hold a blessed amount of 'belief,' regardless of life's trials and tribulations ,it is a miracle in its self, after all my numerous battles within the physical world. The spiritual elements have always helped and compensated. It was a learning to succumb each time, to what I know now, of the greater power and knowledge.

Now that I had visited the Shrine at Knock and had that inner peace restored yet again, there was now a want in me, to visit the ultimate in Shrines, Lourdes, this in turn, would be yet another place where my petitioning prayers would be offered up.

I had no doubt it wasn't just the influence of my religious upbringing but the intermittent influence of my Nun Spirit Guides, Therese and Bridget accompanied by their adoration of Mary the Blessed Virgin too, as they seem to remind me every now and then, just when I think they have stepped aside for a 'too long' a period. I'm then 'drawn' into an element of their earthly Catholic world, they once had.

For if only, it reminds me, to walk in Gods 'Light' no matter who your ever- loving God is, as God is 'One'.

Planning to go to Lourdes was always on a 'back burner', as my family's needs were paramount.

It was, a decade or so later the opportunity came to visit Lourdes, when excess monies from a totally unexpected 'source', arrived with perfect timing. It was one of those 'instrumented' moments of impulse that I booked my flights and hotel for a four day stay with my teenage Granddaughter to keep me company. I was 'lucky' I got a hotel within a two minute walk from the side entrance to the Shrine.

I had so many good reasons for petitioning prayers, and so many people to prayer for; I didn't know where to begin.

I'd heard so, so much about Lourdes and its Miracles. I wanted to make my own mind up about the place and see if I would have any reaction in a physical, psychical and spiritual sense. I wasn't putting my faith to the test. I was just living in hope as usual.

What first impressed me was the sheer numbers of people that seemed to invade such a small village, creating a great amount of 'energy' about the place that didn't seem to fit.

It wasn't long after settling in at the Hotel that I entered the grounds to the Shrine. I had to pass through the crowds that sat in the Square outside the beautiful Basilica. I was eager to see 'Our lady's' Grotto first, which seemed situated at the side. I could hear people in the distance chanting in Latin, repeatedly, a language I'd last heard from my infant years.

I turned the corner to were even greater crowds of people were sitting, kneeling and praying at the foot of the statue of Mary, this was set high up, within the rocky surface of the hillside, where the famous healing waters flowed.

I was aware that I had just 'stepped into' an overwhelming atmosphere. Which, I could only describe as beautiful. There was a serene, presence that seemed to filter, into the core of my being, my soul and by the look and actions of the people, they too were aware, as tear-filled eyes glistened in refection amidst a regiment of lit candles. Their look of fixation said it all.

I stood on the peripheral and observed the protocol and soaked in the 'energy'.

I took pen and paper out my bag and wrote my first prayer petition. I queued up and followed the tradition. I lastly, blessed myself whilst standing under the statue and then returned to my place.

I seemed more engrossed trying to absorb the whole ambience of the place. It was not like I was having a 'solitude' moment with Mary's statue. I found by the end of the first day I'd been was too busy trying to physically take everything in from my new surorundings.

I made a brief plan to visit the Shrine daily at certain times, taking plenty of pen and paper with me.

So I could sit amidst the 'presence' and find some order to my petitioning prayers, so in my mind, I planned to start at the very beginning of my life's journey and go through each decade and put into place a prayer for each person or situation that has graced my pathway, particularly, those people who left significant impressions, whether they were good, bad or in need.

I planned to tell my life story, whilst in a meditative state of prayer to an audience of one, Mary.

So as you can imagine I sat for long periods, nearly three whole days, meditating on the subject whilst sat under the statue of 'Mary the Blessed Virgin' 'Our Lady.'

Writing one prayer request after another I eventually felt like a 'postman', holding a mass of spiritual mail , with that many pieces of folded paper.

The time came to deliver them into the box and receive the Blessing, whilst under the statue.

My granddaughter did her best to follow suit and trailed behind me. I stood for a while contemplating at Mary's feet.

It wasn't until my Granddaughter asked, quiet innocently " Why, are you crying Nanny?"

I realised my face was soaked with tears, yet I hadn't felt any emotion at all. I understood some sort of soul 'cleansing', a healing, was taking place. For that, I felt eternally grateful.

At one stage during my stay I thought I'd have a 'bored' teenager on my hands but my Granddaughter was golden and very patient, but I had no doubt she was in 'awe' of her dwellings and the sheer 'presence' too. Although she didn't fully understand the deeper meaning to its 'existence' but it did have a very positive effect on her.

She became a witness to yet another inexplicable incident, that she agreed, there was no real explanation to…but only that of a 'spiritual' nature.

It was on the third day when we set out to go to Mass, which was being held in the Square outside the Basilica.

We found ourselves lining up along the roadside with the crowds, for quite some time, as they each day gave way and waited in respect, for the procession of royal blue Pram- shaped carriages, carrying the most vulnerable, sick, disfigured, disabled and disadvantaged people of all. They were being pulled along by Nuns, Nurses and Carers alike. They were on the way to take up their 'specially' allocated places at the front of the Shrine.

Some of them were a totally pitiful sight, barely recognisable with disfigured faces and bodies; some seemed almost lifeless, and some making unrecognisable sounds.

But it was when a carriage was aligned with us, I could see there was a disfigured young man lying inside curled up like some wounded delicate creature. It was at that moment that I was convinced I'd heard my name being called. I dismissed it, but no sooner I did, my Granddaughter gave out a squeal of disbelief and shock. She grabbed onto my arm as If the 'unknown' had frightened her.

" Ooh Nanny how does he know your name!?" she squealed.

She'd heard it too, so clearly. Maybe it was a response to the 'cleansing' I'd had the day before.

I reassured her by smiling and giving her a hug, saying

"Well now Michaela, isn't that wonderful?... that's the 'miracle' of Lourdes"

It was a while before she refrained from calling Gods name but the 'experience' no doubt would stay with her forever. (She was in awe and full of surprise and wonder but so proud to tell her R.E teacher at School all about it, on our return).

We met a number of friendly people during our stay there, who shared their own stories of faith with us. Stories of 'healings', and the good reasons given, for their return visits, to give thanks, all understandably so. It was the morning of our last day in Lourdes, an elderly Irish lady recommended that, we shouldn't leave Lourdes until we have had a 'full' Blessing, a submerging in the 'baths' which was filled with the 'sacred' spring water.

Without giving much away, she mysteriously said "Something happens to some people but not all,... let us know how you get on".

I was intrigued to say the least and wasted no time to go and get submerged.

There was a number of singular baths not much bigger than standard bath you have in your home. There was ladies assisting you, as you were wrapped in a cloth and held as you climbed down the few steps into the waist high water and walked a couple of metres to the end, where a small statue of 'Our lady' stood. It was all so quick, I blessed myself, turned round and headed back towards the steps. It was as I was taking the wet cloth off and I was about to dry myself. It was then, I found, I wasn't actually wet to touch, in fact I was dry. Was it some mineral in the water causing this reaction, I thought. Or was it the 'mystery' that I had been told about. It was confirmed later by the Irish lady, the latter was true and then confirmed again by others I met and questioned, and strangely enough by my daughter in England, who I'd phoned that evening. Before I could get to the point about what happened in the baths, she interrupted me and said

'Stop there mom, I know what you're going to say'… You came out dry, didn't you?

She'd 'piped me to the post' in her new found knowledge it seemed.

"Oh I'm surprised you know …. Where did you hear about that?

"I only heard about it this morning. It was a friendly old Irish lady who'd come to buy and collect one of my puppies. She chatted for a while, she asked about my children. I told her you had taken my daughter to Lourdes and then she began telling me how 'wonderful' it is, she mentioned the 'Baths', hence me knowing about the 'water','' she explained.

'Wonderful' it is and I couldn't agree more.
It seems there was no coincidence, to the fact, that the story of the 'mystery' was being 'duplicated' at the same time that morning.
I left Lourdes feeling learned, refreshed, cleansed and well Blessed to say the least. 'Our Lady's blessed influence and intercessions continue to impress and bless, not only my life but all who come and succumb to her. My Marian 'impressions' would no doubt continue to be, although I might need reminding at times in profound and subtle ways.

Revisited II

No more so, than out of the mouth of a Nun came a truth, a Sister of Mercy, in fact, who I had a totally unexpected meeting with. It was after a diversion on the motorway which was leading me towards Liverpool City, but on a total new course.

My youngest daughter was accompanying me. I found myself driving through an area which seemed so 'distantly' familiar. I pointed out that Woolton was the area where the Convent Children's home was, where myself and siblings frequented during a turbulent time in my early chilldhood. My 'sensitive' daughter had heard it being mentioned on the occasion. I didn't need to explain anything more.

Driving along, I noticed some big rusty wrought iron gates, that was set on a corner of a road, these looked as if they hadn't been used for some time, as the positioning of them were not exactly traffic –friendly. I slowed down and took a look through the bars, at an overgrown patch of wilderness that looked as if it had once aligned a driveway. Images began to unravel in my mind exactly, what place it was, this was confirmed as I spotted the legs of a woman, amidst the over grown bushes, wearing a navy pleated calf length skirt. Her being there, just didn't quite fit the equation but her attire gave it away.

I almost shouted at my daughter as I told her

' That's it, that's the Convent and that's a Nun" I exclaimed almost shouting on impulse.

"And were going in I stated. There must be another entrance somewhere?" I said, searching.

We found it. It adjoined the original entrance, a little way down the road.

Then the silence between the two of us spoke volumes. My daughter must have been picking up on my feelings, as we drove slowly up the winding driveway.

The driveway opened up to a full view of a Grande Georgian Mansion house, which once was a dark and dingy grey building, now it had been painted an unrequited 'glorious' white. There it stood with its mountainous steps leading up to a broad oak doorway, held up by majestic Roman pillars. There seemed no indication of any sign explaining to what it was now.

I parked up. I glanced round at the spacious tidy grounds. I could only spot two other cars.

My daughter gave me a gentle nudge to encourage me to investigate, as she 'knew' this was something I had to do alone. I had to close a 'door' in my mind, once and for all.

My stomach churned a multitude of times in its very pit. I rang the doorbell once, which took a lot of courage and I waited, for what seemed the longest time.

I started to feel detached and empty.

The very large oak door opened so far and the head of a wrinkled old Nun peered through the gap that she had gaged and held on to. She looked at me with suspicion.

Yes can I help you" she said rather abruptly.

" Er er erm could you tell me whether this was a childrens home at one point in time? I said stuttering.

I don't know why I asked that but it was a starting point.

She looked me up and down almost rigorously, as if she was trying to make judgement.

She concluded her thoughts and answered herself as she asked

'Are you one of the children? We seem to have a lot of them, who come looking"…what for? What I don't know' she stated and asked herself

Her lack of 'sensitivity' just summed up a 'culture' of an 'old Regime'. My body took a step back. She went on to explain that the building was now a Nursing home for elderly Nuns.

After a another scrutinizing look at me. I was surprised she invited me in.

She asked me specific details about names, dates and time periods and stated that she didn't think any of the present retired nuns, would have been there at the times I'd stayed.

She then, ordered me to wait in the Hallway as she suggested a cup of tea was necessary. By this time her voice seemed to 'echo' even more, with her present 'air of authority' she'd shown. She then disappeared through a door.

I was left alone. I was conscious I was standing on that same spot I once stood, rooted in fear, for a second time.

It felt that my physical being had shrunk.

I began scanning every nook and cranny of my surroundings from a lower level with the eyes of that once fearful child that had been kept, so distant and deep within me. My soul was being touched, 'transported' back. The plush carpet under my feet, had disappeared and the coldness of the old stone floor crept into my bones. 'The 'Sacred Heart' statue that stood in the centre of the large reception hall seemed to tower above and over me, 'watching' me.

I was back in time, reliving a moment, when all my young fears and 'senses' were being 'alerted' for the very first time. I could smell a combination of carbolic soap and a remaining 'essence' of boiled potatoes and defused candles.

I could hear the rustling of starched garments and the chinking of rosary beads, the flapping of headdresses, carried by hurried clockwork footsteps which didn't seem to stop, in the never ending corridors, which had the sounds of doors closing and locking behind them, but never seeming to open to the sounds of whimpering children.

All of which I sensed, came hand in hand with a multitude of closeted emotions. I was engulfed in a total cloak of fear and helplessness.

Internally, I was back in the turmoil, my stomach had churned up suppressed feelings attached to a time when a day felt like a year, more so, when you are in trapped shock of your surroundings. I stood 'frozen' to the spot.

I hadn't flinched until, I could see the Nun approaching, carrying a tray of tea. I was aware my 'pan face'- look, was now on display, a face that seemed to be a contagious epidemic, a learned trait in children, in such circumstances and institutions.

A guise that I'd held all my life, as I couldn't give away to others what I really 'felt' and 'saw' that was too much to confess. After all I had to survive. But never the less I always 'felt' someone was helping me. The pan- face look that Ioften mirrored from the other children, helped to hide all that was truly going on inside but I understood it fundamentally developed as a result of institutionalized oppression. I was fortunate to be blessed later in developing a 'good sense of humour' that became a coping mechanism too, as Id often try to deflect deep emotional feelings with humour on occassions.

I then made an effort to smile at the Nun on her return.

The nun lead me into an office and sat me down and offered me, my cup of tea.

She seemed to ask me a lot of questions. I felt I was being assessed to what my 'motive' was.

There was no mention of an offer to show me around. Her lack of sensitivity was expressed by being so surprised that I knew almost every brick of the place as I described the outlay to the whereabouts of certain rooms to her.

She asked how my life had been since leaving the Convent. I couldn't begin to tell her about my soul's journey as it has been so 'colourful' or about

the experience in Convent Care.

I briefly told her about the amount of times I'd survived life's traumas and how each time 'I'd turned to my self- discovered 'belief system, my 'faith' which had grew and developed alongside each of those times.

I was reminded once again of Mary's impression, as

the Nun glanced down at my hand and recognised the design on my ring, a ring I'd worn on my finger for many decades, which was bought after I had 'survived' another remarkable incident, a serious car crash.

The ring depicts yet another story of Mary's miraculous Intercession).

With raised eyebrows and pointing to my ring she said.
' Erm…I see your wearing the ' Miraculous Medal', then.'
After listening, to a small summary of my life's events.,
She went on….. 'you haven't 'survived' life as such, you have been saved." she acclaimed.
I needed to hear that at that moment, it felt good to know, that Mary's 'influence' was still parallel and would continue to embark on such moments of want and despair, not only for me but for people I have encountered on my journey, sometimes within, surprising, aspects of my 'spiritual' work, which has no set boundaries to creed, culture or religious beliefs as we are all connected to the same God.
My 'soul' felt a little 'lighter' when I left. I was happy to close that big 'oak door' on my past. But it didn't stop me making another visit some months later. I had to 'test' my 'senses' once more. Again I was invited in. This time it was different, as when I walked in, my 'soul' stood tall and undisturbed. Memories and feelings hadn't been forgotten but I had no doubt 'sensed' a 'healing' had taken place.

People and places are sometimes 'Blessings in disguise,' which in some ways help to define who we are, and who we are meant to be, they certainly add to our souls DNA and is woven into the 'fabric' of our soul's journey.

Two Crosses

Part of my make-up has being able to relate a specific past experience, to whomever I'm dealing with in my daily spiritual work, as there is a set pattern in life, that seems to present circles within circles at times. I often meet a kindred spirit who has had similar experience. They have come 'seeking' as they.ve not yet found reason or purpose to why certain things happen and is seeking some sort of answer to how it fits into a 'greater picture'. I don't confess to have all the answers as I am an instrument and can only give what I 'receive' and that is to give you what your soul needs to know with sealed permission.

Not just validation but 'glimpses' of the future and concrete answers too. There always seems a backup up of some anecdotal evidence attached too, that will come to the forefront of my mind., knowing that it is inspired and encouraged to be told by 'spirit'. So it will give people who are seeking, further confirmation and evidence in answers needed to questions, that can bring a definite solace to their soul's request.

My impulsive reactions following spiritual 'instructions' sometimes play a major part in what follows, that is what is 'meant to be' and set in stone.

Martin was one such fellow 'seeker' on a quest for a true 'understanding' of life.

We first met some years ago, after he called, and asked me to visit his home, as he said he had 'strange things going on' and wanted some sort of explanation, confirmation, maybe reassurance and a welcomed blessing too. He wasn't giving much away.

On my arrival I sensed a lot of 'spirit' energy around the house, which sometimes comes with older property's, where there can be layer upon layer of residual 'energy' present.

I sensed his brother had passed away in the property but I did not receive any specific communication from him, although I sensed the specific area where he'd taken his last breath and I felt compelled to relay that he was now at true peace. We spent some time talking about all aspects of spiritual matters, as Martin had a lot of questions he wanted answering, which I gave, we chatted like 'old souls' meeting after an abundance of lifetimes. Some of his life experiences, likes and dislikes had mirrored mine. There were many coincidences which made us in awe of wonder about them. We laughed and almost cried.

Martin smiled at the fact that the love of Rod Stewart was mutual, as I confessed to first seeing Rod with his band the Faces in concert for a 'heavenly' price of £1.75p back in 1973 and that I, still somewhere, had got the concert ticket stub which I'd saved as a memento of my teen years.

(Little did I know that the concert ticket stub would become so much more memorable years later.)

Martin, it seemed, was a man of many colours, a real character. He at first, gave you the impression that he was very much a macho man, a man's man, very down to earth and very proud. He'd had what 'appeared' to be a 'Bachelor's' lifestyle. He was an ex-soldier, brave in service but later battled bravely, a number of episodes of ill health. There were many sides to his personality. He was an avid fan of Manchester United Football Club. He loved his music, and was a very unmistakable fan of Rod Stewart and at one point in his life, had been a 'Rod' impersonator'. He was charming and entertaining, the ladies just loved him. He was known to many as 'George' a nickname he acquired, which was rooted in the humorous fact, that he called everyone 'George' regardless of creed colour or gender. In fact he had a hidden 'sensitive' side, amidst the charade of his popular existence.

The true love of his life was his only child, his daughter Kerry, who he absolutely adored and she him. He had a genuine love of people and animals, a natural empathy particularly for those less fortunate. He was generous with his 'gifts' and his time.

He definitely had a true passion for almost every aspect of life and a strong thirst to understand more of its true meaning.

I sensed that at times he unknowingly, expressed a lot of 'light' into the world around him.

He was the sort of man who always 'touched' people in some way and left an everlasting 'impression,' you could say he had 'charisma' but it was his added 'spirituality' that made him shine, although he wasn't aware of the full extent of the 'light' he was shedding throughout his journey, that I had no doubt.

All it takes is faith the size of a mustard seed. God loves a 'seeker', and that's what Martin surely was.

There was a deeper 'knowledge' within him, that he'd felt, had always been there. That inner 'knowing' was something he had difficulty in expressing, especially in his younger years. Maybe it was through his 'naivety', lack of understanding, and circumstances, which made it difficult to express his spiritual side earlier on.

There were not many people he could express these kind of thoughts and feeling too, not even members of his close family. He'd always felt like a 'square peg in a round hole' with his beliefs, so he confessed. He had been bought up in a large family, a family who were not particularly, practicing any type of religion as such but a loving one never the less.

He loved his close and extended family, so dearly. Although he often said he 'felt' different and sometimes separate, as he knew deep down there was something more to this 'physical' life. In recent years he began to 'express a belief and love of 'Angels' .as their popularity not necessarily in a 'religious' sense grew.

Anyone seeing the statues of Angels scattered about his home would be surprised by it, it certainly gave a different impression, of what he expressed in his, 'male dominated world' outside the four walls.

He so much wanted to know more, about the concept of God, Jesus, an Afterlife and the Spiritual Realms. At times he felt so insecure about what he knew, but gained some comfort from the 'seeds' that was set in his souls DNA, although his beliefs faltered at times due to his questionable faith. He never, truly gave up searching for 'answers', answers he needed, for a peace of mind.

It was obvious to me, he had a very deep spiritual side to him, deeper than what he knew and understood but he hung on to those dim lit foundations never the less.

But I knew he was meant to be placed where he was in this life, as it was all a part of his souls journey, to leave 'impressions' of light on people and maybe leaving a legacy behind later, of some sort, I thought.

The seeds of our 'spiritual' connection had been sewn together by the long lasting 'impressions' we shared each other back in the past.

We rekindled that connection some years later by the introduction of the technical 'social' media site Face book.

It was after a recent move of property, I was unpacking boxes and fell across some football memorabilia, that I no longer had wall space for, as I had downed sized my home.

It was strange how Martin came to mind, as I unpacked mementos of the legendary footballing Genius George Best. I hadn't seen Martin for a number of years.

I just 'knew' he would be interested in them but I really being instrumented to think that. .

I 'messaged' him on social media. We 'connected' once more. But this time it turned out to be for the greatest and deepest purpose. For what was about to unfold, was the 'real' reason to our first 'spiritual connection' that was made all those years ago, when we first met.

Martin told me to 'hold fire' with the memorabilia, as he had an upcoming meeting with a Hospital Consultant and that the result of which, could be life changing so he informed me.

It was a week or so later he text me to tell me he had Cancer and he in his 'doubt' inevitably felt and expressed that his time on earth was coming to an end. I was saddened to hear him say such words. I gave him words of encouragement. Never the less the 'soldier' within him said he had decided to battle whatever was planned and set before him. I myself even battled with my thoughts and feelings I was receiving.

Martin asked if I would come and visit him at home as he said he needed a sitting and more importantly some healing. Hope was all he had. He was relatively housebound due to initial medical procedures; I arranged my visit a few days later.

That allocated, evening before I left my home, I'd said a quick prayer or too, whilst I was dashing around round, running late as usual. I was conscious I wasn't thinking too deeply or so I thought. I just quickly

asked my Angels to brace my emotions, by placing on my usual 'set of armour', and asked them to guide me and uphold me.

As I went to grab my coat, from the hallstand, I was stopped in my tracks. I found myself looking up above the front door where a small blue Crucifix hung.

It was then I heard a 'lady's' voice in my thoughts, so clear and serene.

As she said 'Give this Cross to Martin.'

Without the need for repetition, question or doubt, I 'knew' I was being totally 'instrumented, as I went and got stepladders and took the Cross down and placed it in my pocket. I was just doing as I was told.

Unbeknown to me at that time, this cross was going to play a major part in Martin's journey.

I arrived to a warm welcome from Martin, we sat and chatted for a while about his condition and the plans to start his Chemotherapy and then made small-talk about, all and sundry.

We sat in the living room amongst his prominent display of Angels and Rod memorabilia. I suddenly felt an overwhelming presence fill the room.

It was Martins loved ones in spirit wanting to communicate.

I spoke totally instrumented.,

"Martin your loved ones are all around you, there here now. There are three of them, that are drawing close to you. It's your father, your mother and your brother. It is your father I sense first. He had a connection with the Army, early on in his life. He was a hardworking man. I can 'see' him on a black bicycle with his lunch bag across his shoulder riding up the Pleck Road towards a factory.

Martins face lifted with gentle smile as he confirmed that his father had once worked in a factory on the Pleck Road. I told him his father's spirit was helping to give him strength at this time. His brothers 'energy' stepped into the equation too, when I was compelled to say the words inspired by his spirit alone.

His brothers words were:

'Lost and found!, lost and found!? I repeated. 'What does he mean? I asked Martin.

Martin confirmed that his brother was a bit of a wanderer and he hadn't seen him for a number of years and after a search, he found him and they were reunited but shortly after that, his brother died unexpectedly and tradgecally. He explained.

"Martin, he wants to say he is so glad to of been near his family when he died and to thank you for finding him BUT there was nothing you could do to change things" Martins eyes filled with tears. I sensed Martin felt some kind of guilt, thinking he failed in an opportunity to change things, but the fact is our entire journey is really 'set in stone', as we go by the Grace of God. Martin so needed to know this.

It was then; I felt the surge of his Mothers love, I sensed his mother's spirit envelope him. As she place her arms around him.

" You were the baby in the family weren't you Martin?, so I hear." I said. He nodded.

"Your mother loves you so, so much. She's so full of pride and joy for you. She mentions Holland? Why's that?" I asked.

"Mom would speak a lot about Holland. Mom was actually Dutch. She and Dad met during the war. He explained.

"What's this about, a Cross?" I asked. I knew that it wasn't the cross in my pocket that was being referred to. I let Martin explain.

"I thought it was strange, as I found a cross in Moms belongings after she had passed. I never thought she was religious, but I kept it. I carry it in my wallet. I'll show you, I'll go and fetch it" he said.

He hurried out the room.

He came back with his fist clenched tight, holding his treasure, something that had given him an element of faith in its discovery. He opened his hand.

I gasped at the sight. I told Martin to just stop there in his tracks and be quiet, as I have something to tell him and show him.

I told him about the 'Lady's' message I'd heard, just before leaving the house. I pulled the Cross out of my pocket and held it beside his in his outstretched hand. Miraculously, they matched up, both blue Crucifixes, and an almost replica in design of each other. His 'faith' and beliefs had been sealed.

Martin fell to his knees and broke down uncontrollably at the sight.

"I so believe now, Ange, you've made me believe" he said repeatedly.

Surrounded by his loved ones in spirit, He held onto the crosses, one in each hand, as we prayed together for peace and healing, in Jesus's name.

Martin became somewhat elated, and repeatedly said he could feel heat and a peace passing through his body.

I knew, once more, a souls 'healing' through the Holy Spririt was taking place, and no matter what the outcome of the time ahead would be. It was all in Gods sheltering and deciding hands.

We went on to chat, about many things, mostly of a spiritual nature, I told him of my 'experiences' of Mary

'Our Lady' and my visits to Knock and Lourdes. He was intrigued and obviously 'spiritually' thirsty.

I left him that evening in a state of true Peace and in awe of Gods wonder and in a newfound solace state to except whatever was going to be God's will.

It was days later, he sent me a photograph from his hospital bed, as he prepared himself to battle his first session of chemotherapy, with his Crosses in hand and my book to read, to keep him occupied, he thanked me and told me I made him a true 'Believer' now, without any doubt.

I sent along, prayer cards, inspiring words and songs via text to help him. One such song I just happen to come across, which was quiet apt and synchronized without doubt. It was 'Angel' by Rod Stewart and the Faces. It was actually an old clip on a you tube video of the concert I had attended all those decades ago, the one I had mentioned and still had the concert ticket stub to.

The weeks that followed weren't without questions, but it wasn't for the fact he ever doubted his beliefs. He text me and asked about the practicalities of maybe visiting Lourdes for a blessing at some stage, he was hoping to take his daughter with him.

It was during one of his hospital sessions that I received an unexpected text.

He said he'd had just a strange experience and began to explain that a woman, had walked into his room, as he lay on his bed dozing. He said the woman knew his name and of his condition. She asked if he believed in

God and Jesus and would he mind so much if she said a prayer for him. He told her he believed in Jesus and that he welcomed her prayers. He said she went and drew the curtains and then sat and held his hand and prayed, just as if she was talking to Jesus directly and as she did, he said he got that warm wonderful feeling of peace and pure love, once again, that was undoubtedly of the Holy spirit sort, which passed through his body, and then she got up to leave. Martin asked her name, she replied and she left almost as quickly as she had arrived. It all seemed like a dream to him. He got off his bed and opened the door quickly and watched her walk away. She seemed to ignore other people and patients, as if her only intentions were to visit him alone, He explained.

" It might have been the Hospital chaplain"

(and I had thoughts about thanking her).

I asked Martin what her name was. What he said didn't surprise me.

"She said her name was Marian.' came the reply.

What an uncanny coincidence or should I say there is no such thing at all.

"Its's all in the name, take it as a true and special Blessing".I reminded him.

In the months ahead, Martin appeared to climb a mountainous range of emotions involving the six sessions of chemotherapy, each one became an 'Everest' to 'conquer' and he typically celebrated each one with a 'hearty cheer' as he accomplished one at a time with great courage and armed with the faith that the 'two crosses' gave him, as he held them one in each hand each time.

It was within the last part of his treatment, the Radiotherapy, he text me, to arrange a meeting for the following week. I then received another text hours later, to say that he did not feel well at all, and that he was being admitted to another Hospital for further investigations and that he'd be in touch soon. My heart sank. My spirit knew things; I was too upset to admit to. I sent him many an encouraging message. But it was a day or so later. Unmistakeably Martins spirit sent me a solid message' in the most likely form. I woke up to find an 'Apport', which was an undoubtable sign from Martin.

It was the Faces concert ticket stub was inexplicably but strategically placed. I found it lying in the centre of my living room floor. I picked it up and examined it. I rubbed my eyes as if I could adjust my sight in some way. The ticket was real and it had been placed there. I held it and stared at it for a while. I then heard Martin's voice in my mind saying…..

"Thank you, Ange…but I have got to go now" he spoke in a contented tone. I sat and cried, just in 'the knowing'.

My 'Angel' Friend had returned home to the Heavenly Realms. There was no sudden shock amidst my tears, when I soon heard the 'news 'from his relatives that he'd passed over.

Martin was now in a place he knew and loved so well, surrounded by all his loved ones, he held so dear, but in the hands of Gods loving care most of all

I received an unexpected text from his daughter Kerry Thanking me, for playing an important part in her father's last days, she mentioned how the two crosses played a pivotal important part too, as they had given him so much comfort. I was overwhelmed once more. Kerry had plans to place the crosses with him. But Martin had other ideas, so it seemed.

It was a few days after, Kerry, contacted me again in shock, to say she couldn't find the crosses. She was panicking. There seemed no explanation as to why she couldn't find them. She said she had placed them inside her handbag not long after his last breath, as she knew how much he felt about them. She became terribly upset at the thought of them being lost. I sensed she was hoping I'd used my 'Psyche' to find them or maybe a message from her Dad.

Little did she know that my thoughts and words were actually being 'instrumented' as I told her.

"They're not lost as such. You will find the crosses but not until after the funeral, as your father wants them to remain here, as a permanent reminder of the true Faith that he found.

I felt she couldn't absorb what was being said as it seemed she lived in hope of discovering them in time.

But, so, it was to be, that the two crosses were found, or shall I say just as 'spoken', they did reappear but only after the funeral day had gone by.

Kerry's funeral plans for her father, were meticulous, every ounce of her energy and love was expressed into every small detail, it seemed, she wanted to portray and 'celebrate' every aspect, of her loving father's colourful personality and life.

Kerry must have been totally overwhelmed, as much as I was, as so many were too, by the sheer numbers of unexpected people that had turned up to pay their last respects. The streets were aligned, as there was no room in the Church. People had travelled the length and breadth of the country. Each had heart-warming stories to tell, on how Martin had 'touched' their lives in some way, shape or form. I knew Martin's spirit was beaming with pride, as he watched over 'his' day.

There was an unmistakeable expression of Stewart Tartan which donned many of his floral tributes and button holes. Numerous Members of 'Smiler'- (Rod Stewarts Fan Club had arrived in their droves. Rod Stewart songs were played amidst traditional hymns. The one song that took me by surprise, the most, but in hindsight, I suppose it didn't. It was an operatic rendition of 'Ave Maria' I just knew Kerry must have been 'inspired' to make room for that one.

Kerry did him proud. The day ended with a real 'Celebration' 'Martin style'. As the 100's that stood him proud, remained, as they 'Danced the night away', to the sounds of Rod Stewart and Martins friend, a remarkable Rod Stewart tribute act -.Garry Pease.

Martin will be remembered for many things by many different people.

The 'light' that he shed will remain in the hearts of so many. But it is in his new found 'light' he leaves us with his 'two crosses' that I'm sure he'd want to be remembered for the most.
I pay tribute to him and his memory as he becomes one of 'Angela's Angels' a helper in many ways, now encased in my book forever. God bless you my 'Angel' friend, in all your works. Until the next time!

The line above was once a decisive end to this planned chapter in Martins story, so I thought. But the books file got stuck in a strange manner and along with other distractions in life, the file took a back burner for a while or should I say it stood its time in perfect order for greater reason and purpose, so it seems.
As you, know 'life and love never ends'.

It was some months later on a scheduled Hospital visit of mine, to the same Hospital that Martin had spent most of his last days, that the timing of things became even more apparent.
It was natural for me to think of him as I past his old Ward but it was uncanny when I noticed the

department I was visiting, was next door to the Hospital Chaplains Office.

It was then, in one of my 'instrumented' moments when I found myself knocking on the door. I knew I had to do something for Martin. His memory and presence was inspiring me.

My intention was to thank 'Marian' Martin's unexpected visitor. I concluded she came from the Chaplains office. I knocked the door.

There stood the Vicar before me. I explained in a hurry, the purpose of my call. Hoping he would direct me to Marian.

I was confused for a while after he replied.

'I think you're mistaken, we have no Marian that works here'

I went over the facts again in my head. I then realised what had happened as I said.

'I think I need to tell you something, can you spare a few minutes, please?

He invited me in his office.

I went on as I explained hurriedly, examining it all aghast, but in detail yet again but almost all in one long breath as I said.

'This lady came to his room, she knew his name, she knew of his condition and she asked if he believed in Jesus and would Martin, like her to pray for him. Which he said, 'yes' and welcomed her to do so.

After drawing the curtains, she laid hands on him and prayed over him. He said he felt a wonderful peaceful feeling pass throughout his body. He went on to ask

her name, which she gave reply to. Then she left the room as quick as she had arrived. He followed her out, moments later.
It seemed she had only one intention and that was to visit him, as she disappeared in the distance up the corridor.
He was left feeling dazed, elated and at peace but most of all comforted. He then texted me to tell me of the 'strange and flighting' experience. I made 'light' of her name being Marian as I reminded him of the relevance.

I told the vicar I still had the text on my phone.

'So you see 'father' I said, (using the incorrect terminology to his status but it was something of which I was accustomed to).

'You say she's not from your office but is she some sort of volunteer, then?' I asked.

He replied quite bluntly.
'I know!, ALL! the names of the volunteers in my department, as it is my job to do so, as we have to be very careful, who we send to peoples bedsides'.

We both agreed that the lady 'Marian's' visit , was a mystery. It became even more of a mystery and it was quite fitting, now, to all three of us, as I told the

Vicar the uncanny significance to her name, was something that Martin had only recently accustomed to.

'Even if Marian was a complete Christian stranger, who somehow, had heard about him and took an opportunity to help in a way, she only knew. That was a 'miracle.' wasn't it? I asked.

Martin's 'shared' belief in 'Angels' suddenly sprang to mind.

'Do you think she was an earth 'Angel' or an Angel, that was sent, Father?' I looked to him for some validation.

The Vicar shrugged his shoulders and then with arms apart, he looked upwards with reverence and said

'The good Lord moves in mysterious ways, Angela.'

I had to sit for even more moments, just pondering on the 'wonder' of it all.

Confirmation yet again, of my life-long belief in 'Angels' whether celestial, spirit form or human kind.

I think and I have no doubt that Martin was 'visited' that day, by one of his very own 'beloved' 'Angels'. Don't you?

.

Until the next time ……….. God Bless you 'Ar kid!'

.

MARTIN BAKER

Beliefs

These are some of my personal beliefs and philosophies. Some I have learned through my own personal endeavours, others I have gained through living life with the knowledge of Spirit. These words came to me late one evening while I was beginning what I thought would be a chapter on my beliefs. Instead I was 'given' this prayer, which I'd like to share with you:

I believe in one Almighty GOD. A force, a spirit, energy of infinite LOVE, LIGHT and COMPASSION.
God is LOVE.
LIGHT always overcomes dark.
God is LIGHT.
Light always overcomes dark. God
is SPIRIT.
His spirit can be found in ALL living things.
The power of his spirit is beyond the UNIVERSE.
FAITH is the belief in the 'unseen'. There is no such thing as coincidence. They are God's little miracles.
I believe in MIRACLES.

Nothing is beyond God's power.
I believe in JESUS CHRIST the power of his LOVE and SPIRIT, The HOLY SPIRIT and the Intercession of the VIRGIN MARY, All the ANGELS and SAINTS, and the SPIRIT of our LOVED ONES
RELIGIONS are often devised by man for man's sake, Often telling us that they are the true pathway, there is no singular true pathway but LOVE.
There is a common thread that unites us all and that is LOVE
All religious roads lead to ONE GOD.
Our pathway to God can be found in our inner self – the 'INNER SPIRIT', which connects us to the greater spirit of God.
We are all a splinter of God.
Every second of our lives is MAPPED out.
Everything has 'PERFECT TIMING' and DIVINE PURPOSE.
God holds the blueprint.
We can all be a 'CHANNEL' of his PEACE.
Channels give us comfort and HOPE.
Hope is what we need to survive life's JOURNEY.
Each and every one of us is on a journey of DISCOVERY.
Our soul is sent to the Earth plane to LEARN.
Every soul has a purpose.
Life is an enduring task.
In life there are many LESSONS.
Our BURDENS turn out to be of God's BLESSINGS.

It is not what we learn; it is how we learn.
And it's not about how many problems we have; it is how we deal with them that really counts.
There is no set answer to our problems sometimes, but it is knowing when we are beaten we surrender ourselves to the power of God's word and works – that is when we become a 'LEARNED SOUL'.
Never worry, as worry doesn't change things.
One of the hardest lessons is LOSS.
It is within LOSS that we feel the GREATEST LOVE.
It is then we are the closest to GOD.
We are the closest to GOD in our greatest DESPAIR.
We have not LOST for we have GAINED.
The power of PRAYER is a wonderful thing.
Prayers are our 'asking', MEDITATION is our 'answers'.
All prayers are answered, but sometimes not in 'our' time.
For God has the ANSWER.
There are things we need to know and things that are best left unsaid.
It is when we have to succumb that we are shown the greatness of God's POWER.
I believe in Heaven, a SPIRIT World and Spirit GUIDES.
We are never 'alone'.
There is a spiritual hierarchy of planes that we aspire to according to our soul's development.
I believe in ANGELS, Spirit Guides, highly evolved souls and the ANGELIC REALMS.
We are never so LOST that our Angels cannot find us.
LIFE is the ultimate GIFT.

Children are sent and often lent.
CHILDREN are sent to share and touch our pathway.
COMMUNICATION with the Spirit is also a GIFT.
Some gifts have to be DISCOVERED and NURTURED.
There is no such thing as 'DEATH'. Death is a changing of CONDITION.
BLESSED are those who MOURN.
Our loved ones can communicate to us from the REALMS of Spirit.
I believe in ETERNAL life, the continuation of the soul and REINCARNATION.
I believe in 'KARMIC' forces.
COMPENSATION for all the good we have done and RETRIBUTION for all the bad in this life and the one hereafter.
I believe in ETERNAL LIFE.
But it is THE MIGHT OF GOD'S LOVE THAT CONQUERS ALL.

I want to give thanks to God, my Spirit Guides and helpers for these inspirational words

Afterword

God bless all the wonderful people I have met who have graced my pathway from both sides of life, those beautiful people here and those wonderful souls of the Spirit World, the people of the 'light' whom I have been fortunate enough to meet and help communicate their messages of love and hope, those spirits who have helped me to give encouragement and enact change for those who thought all had been lost.

I am blessed to be able to help to heal and enable people to carry on with their lives each day, knowing that our relationships with our loved ones continue even though the physical body has gone. The loving thoughts we have for them continue into the next world and this enables Spirit to convey and communicate that love, as it never ends. I am blessed in being able to give people the knowledge that each day we are one day closer to our loved ones, who I know we will meet again in God's Kingdom.

I hope this book will be one of many that I write and that it will become part of a legacy for future generations, and for whenever people start question the 'meaning of life' and want to discover the infinite wisdom that life does not end. God's energy, love, spirit, His power infiltrates the universe. It is only when we succumb to the power of God's love, His works and His connection – the spirit that is within us all – that we will be able to embrace, and work with,

God's power. And with that knowledge we will be able to help change the world for the better, as anything is possible with God's love.

I often ask myself, 'Who am I?' I will be many things to many people. You can call me a psychic medium or anything else that seems to fit your understanding of my gift. I am a woman of God who lives in a solid world that blends into a spiritual world of wonderment, a world which never ceases to amaze me. I am just an ordinary woman who is a channel and an instrument, whose life has been enriched with knowledge of the afterlife through a gift of communication that was given to me at birth. This gift had to be discovered and developed through the life lessons and experiences which I had to endure. For it was my destiny.

I have become humbled by a life coloured with moments of despair: a life that at the same time has been touched by the grace of God, his angels and his wondrous works. I often stop and wonder and ask 'God, why me?' For I am, his witness.

I realize now what a 'learned soul' I really am, and how much in this life I have gained spiritually. But I have no doubt, even through life's hardships, that I have been blessed. Now I am even more blessed to be able to share this knowledge with you.

I am just a woman, an infinite spirit who has her own true stories of faith and hope, whose mission in life is to tell the world of the greatness of God's power. My understanding is that the souls of light and spirit whom I was destined to meet are true angels, messengers who have given a message of hope not only to their loved ones but to us all. For they, truly, are 'Angela's Angels'.

Angela's Angels Revisited

'Walk on with hope in your heart and you'll never walk alone.'

Made in the USA
Columbia, SC
10 May 2018